The Field Guide to Emotions

A Practical Orientation to 150 Essential Emotions

Dan Newby and Curtis Watkins

WELCOME

Welcome! We hope that you will use this book as a resource to gain greater understanding of emotions and how they impact so much of our lives. In this book, we have offered you our interpretation of what an emotion is pointing us toward and how our body might be shaped around that emotion. Please use this as a starting point for your exploration, not as a truth to be held onto tightly. If anything we say rings true for you and you find it useful, then we have achieved our objective. If anything doesn't ring true for you, please know that each person experiences the world in different ways and allow your experience to be your first guide and our book your second.

DEDICATION

I dedicate this book to my son Andrew, who taught me,
when he was very young, how my anger impacted his world and mine.
For that, I am eternally grateful.
—Curtis

I dedicate this book to my wife Lucy for her wisdom, love,
and all I've learned from her about my own emotions and about
emotions as a territory for exploration and learning.
—Dan

TABLE OF CONTENTS

PREFACE

This field guide emerged out of a shared interest, professionally and personally, in emotions. We, the authors, like all human beings have had emotional challenges. Some may have bordered on illness, but the vast majority stemmed from our lack of understanding of ourselves and others in the emotional domain. From this perspective, the development of our understanding of emotions as a part of being human and not something we get to choose was of deep self-interest. We wanted to live simpler, more coherent lives.

Professionally, we work as coaches and trainers. Our clients live and work in all parts of the world and in a multitude of cultures. We work with lay people, leaders and coaches to help them develop their skills and self-knowledge. One significant aspect of this development is the area of emotions. Since every human has them and because emotions are, as we understand them, "the energy that puts in action," they are essential for leaders, coaches, and every person to understand and employ in their lives. During more than twenty years of coaching and training, we have discovered that while we've all spent a lot of time and energy on intellectual learning, we've largely ignored learning about emotions. We tend to address our emotions only when we are deeply uncomfortable, and we often do this by going to a professional for counseling. Although this can be helpful, it does not take the place of widespread learning and application in the emotional field, or what could be called Emotional Literacy.

If you turn back the clock by 100 years, the world would look very different in terms of human literacy. If you went back a bit further, you'd get to a time when very few people were able to read or write. Today around 85 percent of humans are literate, which puts language at their service in powerful ways. It allows us to read texts, emails, newspapers, menus, and road signs. It allows us to write texts, emails, books, research papers, and love

1

letters. Literacy is so prevalent that when you enter a restaurant or work-place, it is assumed that you are competent to read and write. Emotions and our knowledge of them stands in the place that language did two hundred years ago. At that time, we were linguistically illiterate; today we are emotionally illiterate. Understanding emotions and learning to use them as a tool is one of the next frontiers in human learning. Emotional competence is steadily growing on the list of competencies required for work, such as the one published by the World Economic Forum. Five years ago, it was absent.

Our claim is that humanity's past interpretation of emotions no longer serves us and, if we want to grow in this area, we need to embrace an interpretation that is practical and useful in everyday situations. We invite you to explore and consider the interpretation we offer in the following pages, and we hope it will reveal hitherto unknown parts of yourself and speed the development of your emotional fluency.

INTRODUCTION

How to use this Field Guide

This book is meant to be used as a reference for coaches, leaders, counselors, or anyone interested in developing their emotional distinctions. It lists more than 150 emotions covering most human experience. You may not be aware you are experiencing these emotions but, if you spend time reflecting on them, you will probably discover they're all familiar. What may have been missing is a way to articulate them. That is one way this book can be of help.

Because the interpretation of each entry includes the etymological root, the information it provides us, its impulse or predisposition, how the body responds to and helps shape emotions, its time orientation, and other elements, each emotion can be explored in various ways. For instance, every interpretation includes a quote to illustrate and put it in context. Reviewing the column that identifies which emotions open us and which close us may help identify an emotion we are experiencing or one we observe in our clients or associates. In this way, the interpretations are multidimensional and can be explored through many avenues.

It's important to understand that every effort to articulate emotions linguistically is only an interpretation. Emotions are not directly visible. We get insight regarding which emotion someone is experiencing by listening to them speak and watching their body and actions. This is true for ourselves as well as for others. For example, we feel a tension in our shoulders and we identify it as anxiety. If our thoughts or "the story we are telling ourselves" is consistent with the meaning of anxiety, then we know that is the emotion. In the opening section, we will discuss this point in greater detail, but it is vital to read this field guide understanding that these are the interpretations of the authors and that yours may sometimes be different. In that case, you will have determined an interpretation that works for you, which we encourage you to do. We welcome your questions, insights, and interpretations. As constant learners, we are always making new connections and refining our interpretations. The ideas you share with us will be part of that process.

There are a number of ways to make use of the following content. One is simply to pick an emotion at random and read through the elements thinking how our interpretation aligns with or informs yours. Another is to select an emotion and, before reading, write your own interpretation or notice which emotions you group it with or confuse it with. You might do the same in terms of time orientation, breath, or one of the other somatic aspects. Once you read our listing, you can cross-reference to the other emotions mentioned.

If you're a coach or someone who professionally works with emotions, this field guide can help clarify your understanding of an emotion either before or after a client session. This not only gives you insight into the situation your client is in but expands the emotions available to you.

There is emerging research that shows our ability to name an emotion helps us regulate it. In other words, just being able to put a name on the feeling makes it more available and easier to navigate and work with. This is borne out by the authors' personal experience, and building emotional literacy is valuable even if for this reason alone.

Enjoy your journey through the rich landscapes you'll find in this world of emotions.

A NEW UNDERSTANDING OF EMOTIONS

All human beings share certain fundamentals; breathing, sleeping, and eating are three. These are aspects of being human that, to some degree, we have the power to choose how or when to do, but we do not get to choose if we do them. Beyond these, there are other core aspects of being human that we sometimes overlook. One of these is that all human beings have emotions. Emotions are not discretionary. That is to say, we do not get to choose whether or not we will have emotions. We are emotional beings just as we are rational beings. Although we individually relate to and express emotions differently, depending on our character, culture, and experiences, that doesn't change the fact that we all have emotions.

Fundamental to understanding what we are suggesting is that all your beliefs about what emotions are and how they work are interpretations. They may be supported by research and experimentation, and you may have accumulated data to "prove" that the belief you are proposing is the one and only truth, but if you dig deep enough, you will see that the way you understand emotions is an interpretation. What we, the authors, are offering is simply another interpretation of the phenomenon of emotions. We are not claiming it is true, but we are endorsing it as useful and practical. Our years of experience as coaches, teachers, facilitators, and consultants have shown us that lacking an emotional interpretation that we can use in everyday situations hampers our ability to engage in life in many ways. It makes us less effective in most things we do. It's often a source of confusion, because if we believe that humans are only rational beings, any event that cannot be explained rationally is not understandable.

If you go to the dictionary for a definition of what an emotion is, you will generally find two statements: "An emotion is a feeling" or "An emotion is an affective state of consciousness." While both definitions may have validity, neither is particularly helpful for understanding what emotions are, what role they play in our lives, what it might mean when we experience them, or how to navigate them. Our claim is that understanding humans as more than "rational" beings allows emotions and moods to be more fully understood as useful tools.

In this ontological interpretation, an emotion is what the etymology of the word suggests: e-motion. It is "the energy that puts you in motion" or "that which moves you." We all can notice the energy that urges us to move faster, change position, or say something we consider important. That energy is the emotion. In this case, "action" and "motion" are distinct from "movement." An emotion such as laziness will make lying immobile on the sofa attractive, which is its particular "predisposition to action." Emotional energy could show up as a reaction to an experience, which would be an emotion, or it could be more long-lasting, in which case we might call it a mood.

Both moods and emotions have the following specific attributes:

- **Emotions are simply "the energy that moves us":** This is a practical interpretation that allows us to value and use them as tools in daily life. When we understand they are our "fuel for action," we see the emotional domain as one worth learning about.
- **Emotions (and moods) are nondiscretionary:** By our nature, emotions are present and are part of our makeup. Every human experiences emotions and moods.
- **Emotions (and moods) are a legitimate domain of learning and knowing:** Whereas previously we believed that learning was primarily intellectual (using language as the carrier of information), our onto-

logical interpretation is that emotions and moods are equal to intellect as domains of learning, knowing, and wisdom.

- **Emotions (and moods) are learned through immersion:** Emotional learning is different from intellectual learning, which happens through insight. Emotional learning occurs through immersion in emotional energy, whether by spending time with our own emotions or by being immersed in the energy of others' emotions.

- **Emotional learning has its own pace**: While cognitive learning happens almost instantaneously, learning in the emotional domain happens over a much longer period of time. It isn't unusual for emotional learning to take weeks or months to take root.

- **We are never not in an emotion:** This is horrible grammar, but it emphasizes the fact that there is never a moment when emotions are not present. We may not be aware of them or able to name which emotions are present, but they are there nonetheless.

- **Emotions can only be known by interpretation:** One can never see emotions directly but can only know them by interpreting how the body senses or displays them, or by the language we use to describe them (which is also a somatic function). Given that, it means that linguistically we can give any particular emotion an interpretation but not an absolute definition.

- **Each emotion or mood predisposes us to a specific action or inaction:** In each distinct emotion or mood, our body is inclined to react in a specific manner. That doesn't necessarily mean we will act in this way, but that the emotions will make us want to act in a particular way.

- **Every emotion is connected with a story or narrative in a co-creative way**: In other words, emotions exist to provide information about our interactions with the world. When I feel ambition, I also am living the story that "there are possibilities for me in life, and I am going to go after them." When I am in the story that "It isn't fair" or "I shouldn't have to," the emotion of resentment is present.

- **Emotions and moods often have a time orientation:** Some emotions are concerned with or focus on the past, some on the present, and some on the future. In some cases, the difference between two emotions is nothing more than this. Regret is the belief that life would have been better if I had made a different choice in the past. Uncertainty is the story that I may make a choice that creates a future I don't like. Peace, serenity, and happiness are concerned with the present. Being aware of this time orientation can help us see if we are living in the present or are more drawn to the past or future.

- **Emotions are not inherently "good" or "bad":** Each emotion can help us or hinder us. When we label emotions as "good" or "bad," we try to avoid the bad ones and get more of the good ones. A more useful question is whether an emotion is serving us in a specific situation.

- **Moods and emotions do not occur one at a time:** We often have several emotions or a combination of moods and emotions in a particular moment. These may be of a similar nature but may also seem paradoxical, such as when we have a love-hate relationship, or we are happy for another's success but also envious of it. One does not contradict the other. Both are telling us something about how we see the relationship.

- **Every emotion takes care of a specific human concern:** Emotions are often thought of as purposeless or as if they simply exist to make us uncomfortable. We believe each emotion developed to take care of a specific human concern. Every emotion exists for a purpose. Loyalty takes care of the groups to which we belong. Guilt takes care of our private identity. Anger tells us what we believe is unjust and gives us the possibility of correcting it.

- **We are not our emotions:** We experience our emotions, but they do not define us. Just as our thoughts are something we can consider and choose not to embrace or believe, our emotions offer us an understanding of the world around us, and thus they are a source of potential understanding. There is a distinction between "us having an emotion" and "an emotion having us."

- **Emotions are triggered; moods are not:** The distinction we draw between moods and emotions ontologically is that emotions are triggered by an event, whereas moods are pervasive energies. What this means is that emotions are provoked by an experience, whereas moods shape the experience we are having. If people live in the mood of fear, they will see the world filled with danger, and that will shape their behavior. If the mood is resentment, they will see the events that happen to them as unfair, because the mood is the lens through which they assess their experience. Put another way: Moods exist before the experience; emotions follow the experience.

- **The existence of emotions is logical:** It may seem paradoxical, but the existence of emotions is logical. If we understand the purpose of our cognitive skills to be the gathering and sorting of information, it is logical that we would need a mechanism to weigh the value of that information. This is the role emotions play in the ontological model.

- **Our emotions are the result of how we're made plus what we've learned:** The eternal "nature vs. nurture" question is evident with emotions and moods. Certainly, we humans are wired in a particular biological way to have the capacity for emotions and individually in the way we process them. And there is a growing body of work that demonstrates how we learn in the emotional domain and how emotions are a part of the learning process.

ACCEPTANCE

ETYMOLOGICAL ROOT

From Latin *acceptare*, "take or receive willingly"

WHAT WE THINK OR SAY

"It is so even though I may not agree, endorse, or like it."

ITS IMPACT ON OUR OPENNESS TO OTHERS

Neutral to opens us

OUR REACTION OR IMPULSE FOR ACTION IS...

To be at peace with what is

RELATED EMOTIONS

Serenity, calmness, peace, contentment

ITS PURPOSE IS TO...

Help us align with reality

THE TIME ORIENTATION OF THIS EMOTION IS...

Present

HOW THIS EMOTION CAN GET IN THE WAY

When fully in acceptance, we have no impulse or capacity to act, which can cause us to miss important aspects of life.

EMOTIONS WE CONFUSE IT WITH

Tolerance, which means "to put up with something until it changes." Acceptance has no such condition.

HOW IT FEELS OR MOVES US

We feel still, without a need to take action.

HOW OUR BODY MIGHT FEEL

Relaxed and engaged

HOW OUR BREATH MIGHT BE

Low in the belly, slow pace, nostril breathing

HOW OUR BODY MIGHT SHAPE ITSELF

Chest is open, belly long and relaxed

QUOTE

"Life is a series of natural and spontaneous changes. Don't resist them; that only creates sorrow. Let reality be reality. Let things flow naturally forward in whatever way they like."—Author unknown

ADMIRATION

ETYMOLOGICAL ROOT

From Latin *admirari*, "to wonder at"

WHAT WE THINK OR SAY

"I would like to do things the way that person does them."

ITS IMPACT ON OUR OPENNESS TO OTHERS

Opens us

OUR REACTION OR IMPULSE FOR ACTION IS...

To emulate or copy

RELATED EMOTIONS

Envy, infatuation, jealousy, adoration

ITS PURPOSE IS TO...

Identify role models

THE TIME ORIENTATION OF THIS EMOTION IS...

Future

HOW THIS EMOTION CAN GET IN THE WAY

If admiration becomes worship, it can lead to infatuation, and we lose the benefit of admiration.

EMOTIONS WE CONFUSE IT WITH

In envy our focus is on "having what the other has"; in admiration it is on "being or doing as the other does."

HOW IT FEELS OR MOVES US

We look up to another and look for ways we can act or become like them.

HOW OUR BODY MIGHT FEEL

Light, tendency to move up and forward

HOW OUR BREATH MIGHT BE

Higher in the chest, more rapid pace, but not fast

HOW OUR BODY MIGHT SHAPE ITSELF

Open chest, smiling, grounded

QUOTE

"I have always been an admirer. I regard the gift of admiration as indispensable if one is to amount to something. I don't know where I would be without it."
—*Thomas Mann*

ADORATION

ETYMOLOGICAL ROOT

From Latin *adorare*, "speak to formally, beseech, ask in prayer"

WHAT WE THINK OR SAY

"I feel divine love."

ITS IMPACT ON OUR OPENNESS TO OTHERS

Opens us

OUR REACTION OR IMPULSE FOR ACTION IS...

To treat with utmost respect or to worship

RELATED EMOTIONS

Affection, admiration, desire, love, passion

ITS PURPOSE IS TO...

Look to a higher power or treat others as such

THE TIME ORIENTATION OF THIS EMOTION IS...

Present

HOW THIS EMOTION CAN GET IN THE WAY

In adoration we can become disconnected from reason and prudence.

EMOTIONS WE CONFUSE IT WITH

Adoration, strictly speaking, addresses our feelings toward a higher power. Emotions such as infatuation, affection, and love are generally directed toward other humans.

HOW IT FEELS OR MOVES US

We pray or ask for guidance.

HOW OUR BODY MIGHT FEEL

Energized and full

HOW OUR BREATH MIGHT BE

Long, slow, and deep

HOW OUR BODY MIGHT SHAPE ITSELF

Head lifted, chin tilted back just a bit, chest open

QUOTE

"The adoration of his heart had been to her only as the perfume of a wild flower, which she had carelessly crushed with her foot in passing."
—Henry Wadsworth Longfellow

ADVENTUROUSNESS

ETYMOLOGICAL ROOT

From Latin *adventura*, "(a thing) about to happen"

WHAT WE THINK OR SAY

"I'm ready for a new experience."

ITS IMPACT ON OUR OPENNESS TO OTHERS

Opens us

OUR REACTION OR IMPULSE FOR ACTION IS…

To explore

RELATED EMOTIONS

Ambition, enthusiasm, curiosity, intrigue

ITS PURPOSE IS TO…

Get us exploring in the world

THE TIME ORIENTATION OF THIS EMOTION IS…

Future

HOW THIS EMOTION CAN GET IN THE WAY

If we frequent the emotion of adventurousness, we may miss the value of routine.

EMOTIONS WE CONFUSE IT WITH

Boldness is required when a situation holds danger and is therefore associated with courage; adventurousness is looking forward to the next thing expectantly.

HOW IT FEELS OR MOVES US

We try out new things or go new places seeking new experiences.

HOW OUR BODY MIGHT FEEL

Engaged, flushed, alert

HOW OUR BREATH MIGHT BE

Faster paced, in upper chest

HOW OUR BODY MIGHT SHAPE ITSELF

Moving forward, eyes wide open, chest open, pelvis and femurs wide

QUOTE

"Life is either a daring adventure or nothing. Security does not exist in nature, nor do the children of men as a whole experience it. Avoiding danger is no safer in the long run than exposure."—Helen Keller

17

AFFECTION

ETYMOLOGICAL ROOT

From Latin *affectionem*, "a relation, disposition; a temporary state; a frame, constitution"

WHAT WE THINK OR SAY

"I like this person and would like to remain close."

ITS IMPACT ON OUR OPENNESS TO OTHERS

Opens us

OUR REACTION OR IMPULSE FOR ACTION IS…

To demonstrate liking or loving through action

RELATED EMOTIONS

Love, passion, desire

ITS PURPOSE IS TO…

Bring us close to others

THE TIME ORIENTATION OF THIS EMOTION IS…

Present

HOW THIS EMOTION CAN GET IN THE WAY

We can experience affection for people who do not have our best interests at heart, which can put us in danger.

EMOTIONS WE CONFUSE IT WITH

Infatuation, which comes from a root meaning "foolish," whereas affection is the state of enjoying another's company.

HOW IT FEELS OR MOVES US

We show we enjoy being in the presence of another person.

HOW OUR BODY MIGHT FEEL

Calm

HOW OUR BREATH MIGHT BE

Even, resting breathing rate medium slow, medium depth

HOW OUR BODY MIGHT SHAPE ITSELF

Open, leaning toward others

QUOTE

"You, yourself, as much as anybody in the entire universe, deserve your love and affection."—Buddha

AGGRAVATION

ETYMOLOGICAL ROOT

From Latin *aggravatus*, "to render more troublesome," literally "to make heavy"

WHAT WE THINK OR SAY

"This is troubling."

ITS IMPACT ON OUR OPENNESS TO OTHERS

Closes us

OUR REACTION OR IMPULSE FOR ACTION IS...

To bear the burden and continue on

RELATED EMOTIONS

Ire, frustration, resentment

ITS PURPOSE IS TO...

Show us what troubles us

THE TIME ORIENTATION OF THIS EMOTION IS...

Present

HOW THIS EMOTION CAN GET IN THE WAY

Aggravation can slow us down and make a chore of what we need to accomplish.

EMOTIONS WE CONFUSE IT WITH

Frustration tells us we think "this could be simpler or faster," whereas aggravation occurs when we have the feeling we are slogging through mud. There may not be a faster or easier way; it is just difficult.

HOW IT FEELS OR MOVES US

We often complain about the difficulty of the situation or burden we feel.

HOW OUR BODY MIGHT FEEL

Tense, flushed

HOW OUR BREATH MIGHT BE

High in the chest, medium rapid

HOW OUR BODY MIGHT SHAPE ITSELF

Leaning forward, closed fists perhaps

QUOTE

"If you have a job without aggravation, you don't have a job."—Malcolm Forbes

AGONY

ETYMOLOGICAL ROOT

From Greek *agonia*, "a (mental) struggle for victory," originally "a struggle for victory in the games"

WHAT WE THINK OR SAY

"What a struggle!"

ITS IMPACT ON OUR OPENNESS TO OTHERS

Closes us

OUR REACTION OR IMPULSE FOR ACTION IS...

To continue trying even though it is difficult

RELATED EMOTIONS

Anguish, dread

ITS PURPOSE IS TO...

Identify our struggles

THE TIME ORIENTATION OF THIS EMOTION IS...

Present

HOW THIS EMOTION CAN GET IN THE WAY

We may restrict our activities, hoping to avoid the pain.

EMOTIONS WE CONFUSE IT WITH

Anguish. Agony is the pain of a struggle, whereas anguish is pain that will not be resolved by winning the battle.

HOW IT FEELS OR MOVES US

We struggle to continue what we have committed to in spite of the pain or difficulty.

HOW OUR BODY MIGHT FEEL

Sharp pain and/or strong dull aches

HOW OUR BREATH MIGHT BE

Short in-breaths, long out-breaths with moans

HOW OUR BODY MIGHT SHAPE ITSELF

Bent over, perhaps in fetal position, depending on the depth of the agony

QUOTE

"I hate and I love. Perhaps you ask why I do so. I do not know, but I feel it, and am in agony."—Catullus

AMAZEMENT

ETYMOLOGICAL ROOT

From Old English, *mæs c.1300, "delusion, bewilderment"

WHAT WE THINK OR SAY

"This is wonderful, and I'm having trouble believing it's real."

ITS IMPACT ON OUR OPENNESS TO OTHERS

Opens us

OUR REACTION OR IMPULSE FOR ACTION IS...

To be entranced

RELATED EMOTIONS

Wonder, awe, incredulity

ITS PURPOSE IS TO...

Expose us to things out of the ordinary

THE TIME ORIENTATION OF THIS EMOTION IS...

Present

HOW THIS EMOTION CAN GET IN THE WAY

Amazement can be pictured as walking around "starry-eyed." In amazement we can lose connection with daily concerns and activities.

EMOTIONS WE CONFUSE IT WITH

Amazement has the quality of confusion as well as unbelievability, and so is different from incredulity, which is simply unbelievability.

HOW IT FEELS OR MOVES US

We are wide-eyed and uncomprehending about the experience we are having.

HOW OUR BODY MIGHT FEEL

Tingling, flushed, energized

HOW OUR BREATH MIGHT BE

Long exhales, medium deep inhales

HOW OUR BODY MIGHT SHAPE ITSELF

Chin lifted, eyes wide open, chest open

QUOTE

"Poetry is the language in which man explores his own amazement."—Christopher Fry

AMBITION

ETYMOLOGICAL ROOT

From Latin *ambitionem*, "a going around," especially to solicit votes

WHAT WE THINK OR SAY

"I see possibilities and want to pursue them."

ITS IMPACT ON OUR OPENNESS TO OTHERS

Opens us

OUR REACTION OR IMPULSE FOR ACTION IS...

To pursue possibilities

RELATED EMOTIONS

Enthusiasm, excitement, zeal

ITS PURPOSE IS TO...

Show us possibilities and give us the energy to pursue them

THE TIME ORIENTATION OF THIS EMOTION IS...

Future

HOW THIS EMOTION CAN GET IN THE WAY

If ambition is the only emotion available to us, we may exhaust ourselves and even damage our health.

EMOTIONS WE CONFUSE IT WITH

Enthusiasm, which means "divinely inspired" or "possessed by the gods," whereas ambition is "seeing possibilities and being determined to capture them" and is thus more focused on earthly pursuits.

HOW IT FEELS OR MOVES US

We go looking for opportunities and looking for ways to take advantage of them.

HOW OUR BODY MIGHT FEEL

Energized, strong

HOW OUR BREATH MIGHT BE

Short, rapid, shallow breaths

HOW OUR BODY MIGHT SHAPE ITSELF

Moving and leaning forward, eyes narrowed and focused

QUOTE

"Intelligence without ambition is a bird without wings."
—Salvador Dali

AMBIVALENCE

ETYMOLOGICAL ROOT

From Latin *ambi-* "on both sides" + *valentia* "to be strong"

WHAT WE THINK OR SAY

"I could go either direction."

ITS IMPACT ON OUR OPENNESS TO OTHERS

Neutral to closes us

OUR REACTION OR IMPULSE FOR ACTION IS...

To follow someone else's lead

RELATED EMOTIONS

Uncertainty, doubt, confusion

ITS PURPOSE IS TO...

Tell us when we are facing two equal options

THE TIME ORIENTATION OF THIS EMOTION IS...

Present

HOW THIS EMOTION CAN GET IN THE WAY

Ambivalence gives us the ability to see the strengths in different possibilities. We can get stuck if we value them equally.

EMOTIONS WE CONFUSE IT WITH

Uncertainty. Ambivalence means we feel equal pulls from opposite positions and are thus stuck; uncertainty means we aren't sure which will have a better outcome.

HOW IT FEELS OR MOVES US

We are immobilized or stuck between two seemingly equal possibilities.

HOW OUR BODY MIGHT FEEL

A bit of tension in the chest and shoulders

HOW OUR BREATH MIGHT BE

Regular, light breathing

HOW OUR BODY MIGHT SHAPE ITSELF

Shoulders shrugged

QUOTE

"We all parent the best we can. Being human, we're ambivalent. We want perfection for our babies, but we also need sleep."—Erica Jong

AMUSEMENT

ETYMOLOGICAL ROOT

Latin from *a* "at, to" + *muser*, "ponder, stare fixedly."
Literally "to muse"

WHAT WE THINK OR SAY

"This is engaging."

ITS IMPACT ON OUR OPENNESS TO OTHERS

Opens us

OUR REACTION OR IMPULSE FOR ACTION IS...

To enjoy

RELATED EMOTIONS

Joy, delight, hilarity

ITS PURPOSE IS TO...

Divert us from difficulties or seriousness

THE TIME ORIENTATION OF THIS EMOTION IS...

Present

HOW THIS EMOTION CAN GET IN THE WAY

Although amusement can be a relief, in excess, it can keep us from the seriousness needed to resolve concerns.

EMOTIONS WE CONFUSE IT WITH

Delight. Amusement has to do with diverting our attention, whereas delight means we are pleased with what we are experiencing.

HOW IT FEELS OR MOVES US

We turn away from serious concerns and allow ourselves to be distracted.

HOW OUR BODY MIGHT FEEL

Relaxed

HOW OUR BREATH MIGHT BE

Light, shallow breaths

HOW OUR BODY MIGHT SHAPE ITSELF

Leaning back and down, open front, slight smile

QUOTE

"Like the bee, we should make our industry our amusement."—James Goldsmith

ANGER

The emotion is.....................

ETYMOLOGICAL ROOT

Latin *angere*, "to throttle, torment"

WHAT WE THINK OR SAY

"This is wrong or unjust."

ITS IMPACT ON OUR OPENNESS TO OTHERS

Closes us

OUR REACTION OR IMPULSE FOR ACTION IS...

To punish the source of injustice

RELATED EMOTIONS

Rage, fury, ire

ITS PURPOSE IS TO...

Identify injustice and, by extension, justice

THE TIME ORIENTATION OF THIS EMOTION IS...

Present or future

HOW THIS EMOTION CAN GET IN THE WAY

Anger is one of the emotions people fear the most, probably because our predisposition is to punish the person we think has done something unjust and, in doing that, we may injure them or our relationship.

EMOTIONS WE CONFUSE IT WITH

Frustration and anger are often seen as inseparable, but anger signals injustice, whereas frustration is our assessment something is taking too long or is too difficult.

HOW IT FEELS OR MOVES US

We look for ways to correct what we consider unjust.

HOW OUR BODY MIGHT FEEL

Flushed, hot, tense

HOW OUR BREATH MIGHT BE

Fast, shallow breaths

HOW OUR BODY MIGHT SHAPE ITSELF

Moving forward and toward, fists clenched, jaw tight, belly tight

QUOTE

"Anybody can become angry—that is easy, but to be angry with the right person and to the right degree and at the right time and for the right purpose, and in the right way—that is not within everybody's power and is not easy."—Aristotle

ANGUISH

The emotion is...............

ETYMOLOGICAL ROOT

From Latin *angustia*, "tightness, straightness, narrowness, to throttle or torment"

WHAT WE THINK OR SAY

"I want to scream because of the emotional pain."

ITS IMPACT ON OUR OPENNESS TO OTHERS

Closes us

OUR REACTION OR IMPULSE FOR ACTION IS...

To struggle for understanding

RELATED EMOTIONS

Agony, sadness, despair

ITS PURPOSE IS TO...

Tell me when the world I know has changed dramatically

THE TIME ORIENTATION OF THIS EMOTION IS...

Present

HOW THIS EMOTION CAN GET IN THE WAY

Because anguish is such an intense emotion, it can challenge others to remain close to us even though their support is needed

EMOTIONS WE CONFUSE IT WITH

Despair. Anguish is provoked by intense loss, so is more related to sadness; despair means to lose hope.

HOW IT FEELS OR MOVES US

We struggle to express or talk about our experience even if we wish to.

HOW OUR BODY MIGHT FEEL

Constricted

HOW OUR BREATH MIGHT BE

Tight, shallow, very high in the chest

HOW OUR BODY MIGHT SHAPE ITSELF

Moving upward, mouth open as if to scream, fists tight, chest tight, belly tight

QUOTE

"Every composer knows the anguish and despair occasioned by forgetting ideas which one had no time to write down."—Hector Berlioz

ANNOYANCE

ETYMOLOGICAL ROOT

From Late Latin *inodiare*, "make loathsome," from Latin (*esse*) in *odio* "(it is to me) hateful"

WHAT WE THINK OR SAY

"I don't like this and wish it would go away."

ITS IMPACT ON OUR OPENNESS TO OTHERS

Closes us

OUR REACTION OR IMPULSE FOR ACTION IS...

To withdraw from participation

RELATED EMOTIONS

Ire, frustration, anger

ITS PURPOSE IS TO...

Tell us what we want to avoid or not participate in

THE TIME ORIENTATION OF THIS EMOTION IS...

Present

HOW THIS EMOTION CAN GET IN THE WAY

Annoyance signals us that something is uncomfortable or bothersome. Sometimes, however, we blame others for our annoyance and lash out at them.

EMOTIONS WE CONFUSE IT WITH

Ire or irritation. Annoyance is etymologically related to hate and thus avoidance. Ire means we want to be finished with it as soon as possible to halt the irritation.

HOW IT FEELS OR MOVES US

We express our dissatisfaction with what is happening and threaten to quit.

HOW OUR BODY MIGHT FEEL

A little tightness in the neck and shoulders

HOW OUR BREATH MIGHT BE

Medium deep sighs

HOW OUR BODY MIGHT SHAPE ITSELF

Turned away, head down and to the side, eyes rolled, shaking of the head

QUOTE

"People who think they know everything are a great annoyance to those of us who do."—Isaac Asimov

ANTICIPATION

ETYMOLOGICAL ROOT

From Latin *anticipatus*, "take (care of) ahead of time," literally "taking into possession beforehand"

WHAT WE THINK OR SAY

"I think something good is going to happen."

ITS IMPACT ON OUR OPENNESS TO OTHERS

Opens us

OUR REACTION OR IMPULSE FOR ACTION IS…

To look forward to an experience

RELATED EMOTIONS

Expectancy, excitement, apprehension

ITS PURPOSE IS TO…

Allow us to look forward to good things

THE TIME ORIENTATION OF THIS EMOTION IS…

Future

HOW THIS EMOTION CAN GET IN THE WAY

Anticipation means we are living the experience of something before it happens. We are preoccupied and not living in the present, which can cause us to miss things of importance.

EMOTIONS WE CONFUSE IT WITH

Expectant. Anticipation actually means we are planning and preparing ahead of time. Expectant means looking forward to something we believe will be enjoyable.

HOW IT FEELS OR MOVES US

We think about the good things that are going to happen and imagine how we'll feel when they do.

HOW OUR BODY MIGHT FEEL

Tingling, slight queasiness in the stomach

HOW OUR BREATH MIGHT BE

Faster pace, then resting, in the upper chest

HOW OUR BODY MIGHT SHAPE ITSELF

Moving toward, head up, chest and arms open

QUOTE

"If pleasures are greatest in anticipation, just remember that this is also true of trouble."—Elbert Hubbard

ANXIETY

The emotion is...............

ETYMOLOGICAL ROOT

From Latin *anxius*, "solicitous, uneasy, troubled in mind," from *anguere* "choke, squeeze," figuratively "torment, cause distress"

WHAT WE THINK OR SAY

"I believe something may harm me, but I'm not sure what it might be."

ITS IMPACT ON OUR OPENNESS TO OTHERS

Closes us

OUR REACTION OR IMPULSE FOR ACTION IS...

To worry

RELATED EMOTIONS

Doubt, fear, anticipation, expectancy

ITS PURPOSE IS TO...

Warn us of possible danger even if we can't identify what the danger is

THE TIME ORIENTATION OF THIS EMOTION IS...

Future

HOW THIS EMOTION CAN GET IN THE WAY

If we do not have a way to break out of our circular thinking or worrying, it can dominate our attention.

EMOTIONS WE CONFUSE IT WITH

Fear and anxiety are both the belief that something may harm us; in fear we can name the thing, while in anxiety we can't.

HOW IT FEELS OR MOVES US

We worry (think in a circular pattern) about the danger and outcome we believe might occur.

HOW OUR BODY MIGHT FEEL

Tightening in the belly, shoulders, and neck

HOW OUR BREATH MIGHT BE

Located in the upper chest area, short and shallow breaths, faster than resting pace

HOW OUR BODY MIGHT SHAPE ITSELF

Moving away, shoulders slightly hunched, brow is furrowed

QUOTE

"Concentration is a fine antidote to anxiety."
—*Jack Nicklaus*

41

APATHY

ETYMOLOGICAL ROOT

From Greek *apatheia*, "freedom from suffering, impassability, want of sensation," from *a-* "without" + *pathos* "emotion, feeling, suffering"

WHAT WE THINK OR SAY

"I am not interested."

ITS IMPACT ON OUR OPENNESS TO OTHERS

Closes us to neutral

OUR REACTION OR IMPULSE FOR ACTION IS...

To avoid getting involved

RELATED EMOTIONS

Boredom, ambivalence, resignation, uncertainty

ITS PURPOSE IS TO...

Save our attention for things we care about

THE TIME ORIENTATION OF THIS EMOTION IS...

Present

HOW THIS EMOTION CAN GET IN THE WAY

Sometimes apathy, or lack of passion, looks to others like "we don't care" rather than "we aren't interested," which is different.

EMOTIONS WE CONFUSE IT WITH

Boredom. Apathy is the lack of passion or interest, whereas boredom means we don't see any benefit in what we are doing and thus look for something more valuable to do.

HOW IT FEELS OR MOVES US

We don't take initiative to express our interest or desire, so let others decide.

HOW OUR BODY MIGHT FEEL

Sluggish

HOW OUR BREATH MIGHT BE

Slow, regular, chest breathing

HOW OUR BODY MIGHT SHAPE ITSELF

Downward and back, shoulders shrugged, chest lightly caved in

QUOTE

"Hate is not the opposite of love; apathy is."—Rollo May

APPRECIATION

ETYMOLOGICAL ROOT

Late Latin *appretiatus*, "to set a price to"

WHAT WE THINK OR SAY

"This is of importance to me."

ITS IMPACT ON OUR OPENNESS TO OTHERS

Opens us

OUR REACTION OR IMPULSE FOR ACTION IS...

To thank

RELATED EMOTIONS

Gratitude, thankfulness

ITS PURPOSE IS TO...

Show us what has value to us

THE TIME ORIENTATION OF THIS EMOTION IS...

Past or present

44

HOW THIS EMOTION CAN GET IN THE WAY

Appreciation of another person can sometimes be confused with affection. Appreciation means we find someone or their actions valuable; affection means we would like to be more intimate with them.

EMOTIONS WE CONFUSE IT WITH

Thankfulness. Appreciation means we believe something has value, whereas thankfulness is to reward or give recompense. Thankfulness is active, whereas appreciation can be silent.

HOW IT FEELS OR MOVES US

We acknowledge the value someone or something has for us.

HOW OUR BODY MIGHT FEEL

Energy is up, body is warm and light

HOW OUR BREATH MIGHT BE

Light, even, low in the abdomen

HOW OUR BODY MIGHT SHAPE ITSELF

Smile, relaxed, open

QUOTE

"Nature's beauty is a gift that cultivates appreciation and gratitude."—Louie Schwartzberg

APPREHENSION

ETYMOLOGICAL ROOT

From Latin *apprehendere*, "to take hold of, grasp." Meaning "fearful of what is to come" is recorded from 1630s, via notion of "capable of grasping with the mind"

WHAT WE THINK OR SAY

"I'm fearful of what is to come."

ITS IMPACT ON OUR OPENNESS TO OTHERS

Closes us

OUR REACTION OR IMPULSE FOR ACTION IS…

To hold on

RELATED EMOTIONS

Expectancy, anticipation, anxiety

ITS PURPOSE IS TO…

Have us proceed with caution

THE TIME ORIENTATION OF THIS EMOTION IS…

Future

HOW THIS EMOTION CAN GET IN THE WAY

Apprehension is similar to anticipation in that we are thinking ahead to what may happen. In the case of apprehension, we are generally expecting something bad to happen, which can produce a mood that distances us from others.

EMOTIONS WE CONFUSE IT WITH

Anxiety. Apprehension means to try "to get hold of something" in order to understand it, because we have a concern it could hurt us. Anxiety is to fear something unidentified.

HOW IT FEELS OR MOVES US

We attempt to grasp or understand something unfamiliar.

HOW OUR BODY MIGHT FEEL

Tight in the neck and shoulders and belly

HOW OUR BREATH MIGHT BE

High in the chest, shallow, faster than resting breath, but not racing

HOW OUR BODY MIGHT SHAPE ITSELF

Tendency to move away, head tilted away

QUOTE

"There are more things to alarm us than to harm us, and we suffer more often in apprehension than reality."
—*Lucius Annaeus Seneca*

ARROGANCE

The emotion is......

ETYMOLOGICAL ROOT

Latin *arrogantia*, "assuming, overbearing, insolent"

WHAT WE THINK OR SAY

"I'm better and more important than other people."

ITS IMPACT ON OUR OPENNESS TO OTHERS

Closes us

OUR REACTION OR IMPULSE FOR ACTION IS...

To look down on, condescend

RELATED EMOTIONS

Hubris, rectitude, righteousness

ITS PURPOSE IS TO...

Feel superior

THE TIME ORIENTATION OF THIS EMOTION IS...

Present

HOW THIS EMOTION CAN GET IN THE WAY

Arrogance often pushes others away because of the tendency to be condescending.

EMOTIONS WE CONFUSE IT WITH

Hubris. Arrogance is to believe one is better than others in a moral sense. Hubris means to believe we are "at the level of the gods" and thus untouchable.

HOW IT FEELS OR MOVES US

We look down on other people and speak to them condescendingly or not at all.

HOW OUR BODY MIGHT FEEL

A little tightness in the neck and shoulders

HOW OUR BREATH MIGHT BE

Breath in the middle of the chest, slightly elevated rate

HOW OUR BODY MIGHT SHAPE ITSELF

Chin tilted upward, standing tall and stiff

QUOTE

"An arrogant person considers himself perfect. This is the chief harm of arrogance. It interferes with a person's main task in life—becoming a better person."—Leo Tolstoy

ASTONISHMENT

ETYMOLOGICAL ROOT

Latin *extonare*, from Latin *ex* "out" (see ex-) + *tonare* "to thunder"; so, literally "to leave someone thunderstruck"

WHAT WE THINK OR SAY

"Unbelievable! Amazing!"

ITS IMPACT ON OUR OPENNESS TO OTHERS

Opens us

-    -

OUR REACTION OR IMPULSE FOR ACTION IS...

Be shocked and still

RELATED EMOTIONS

Awe, wonder, delight

-    -

ITS PURPOSE IS TO...

Make us aware of the uniqueness of an event

THE TIME ORIENTATION OF THIS EMOTION IS...

Present

- -

HOW THIS EMOTION CAN GET IN THE WAY

Astonishment may leave us unable, at least in the moment, to react. We may be immobilized and unable to defend ourselves.

EMOTIONS WE CONFUSE IT WITH

Awe. Astonishment is as if we've been struck by thunder, which may not produce fear but more surprise. Awe is to be afraid or in terror as the result of a profound experience.

HOW IT FEELS OR MOVES US

Thunderstruck, immobile

HOW OUR BODY MIGHT FEEL

Energized, awake, alive, tingling, energy streaming

HOW OUR BREATH MIGHT BE

Fast strong inhale, shallow exhale

HOW OUR BODY MIGHT SHAPE ITSELF

Moving up and back, eyes wide open, mouth open, chest open

QUOTE

"I find to my mixed astonishment that I do dream, but I didn't know it."—Theodore Sturgeon (Dr. Seuss)

ATTRACTION

ETYMOLOGICAL ROOT

From Latin *attractionem*, "a drawing together"

WHAT WE THINK OR SAY

"I want to get closer."

ITS IMPACT ON OUR OPENNESS TO OTHERS

Opens us

OUR REACTION OR IMPULSE FOR ACTION IS...

To move closer

RELATED EMOTIONS

Curiosity, fascination, passion, desire

ITS PURPOSE IS TO...

Bring us closer

THE TIME ORIENTATION OF THIS EMOTION IS...

Present

HOW THIS EMOTION CAN GET IN THE WAY

Attraction, like desire, draws us closer to others or experiences. This can cause breakdowns in a relationship or even generate danger. We all know the illustration of "moths drawn to a flame."

EMOTIONS WE CONFUSE IT WITH

Love. Attraction is the emotion that draws us to other people. Love means that we accept someone as they are and have no desire to change them.

HOW IT FEELS OR MOVES US

We focus our senses on and look for ways to get closer to a thing or person.

HOW OUR BODY MIGHT FEEL

Warm, energized

HOW OUR BREATH MIGHT BE

Slightly elevated rate, more in the chest than the belly

HOW OUR BODY MIGHT SHAPE ITSELF

Tendency to move toward, open, smiling

QUOTE

"The attraction of the virtuoso for the public is very like that of the circus for the crowd. There is always the hope that something dangerous will happen."—Claude Debussy

AWE

ETYMOLOGICAL ROOT

From a Scandinavian source, such as Old Norse *agi* "fright," c.1300, or *aue*, "fear, terror, great reverence"

WHAT WE THINK OR SAY

"This is beyond belief, and it is scary."

ITS IMPACT ON OUR OPENNESS TO OTHERS

Opens us

OUR REACTION OR IMPULSE FOR ACTION IS...

To approach with trepidation

RELATED EMOTIONS

Wonder, astonishment, fascination

ITS PURPOSE IS TO...

Demonstrate the smallness of human dimensions compared to those of the universe

THE TIME ORIENTATION OF THIS EMOTION IS...

Present

HOW THIS EMOTION CAN GET IN THE WAY

If the fear we feel in awe scares us away from the event or experience, we cannot learn from it and appreciate it. It then comes closer to terror, horror, or dread.

EMOTIONS WE CONFUSE IT WITH

Wonder. Awe produces a reverence or terror for a greater power, whereas wonder means we are experiencing a miracle or something we marvel at.

HOW IT FEELS OR MOVES US

We are wide-eyed with a blank expression and stop breathing, waiting for the experience to become clear.

HOW OUR BODY MIGHT FEEL

Energized, a little tightness in the chest

HOW OUR BREATH MIGHT BE

Breath is held and then sharply inhaled

HOW OUR BODY MIGHT SHAPE ITSELF

Tendency to move away, open and in full length

QUOTE

"He who can no longer pause to wonder and stand rapt in awe, is as good as dead; his eyes are closed."
—Albert Einstein

BLISS

The emotion is............................

ETYMOLOGICAL ROOT

Old English *blis*, also *bliðs*, "merriment, happiness, grace, favor," from Proto-Germanic *blithsjo*

WHAT WE THINK OR SAY

"This is profoundly satisfying."

ITS IMPACT ON OUR OPENNESS TO OTHERS

Opens us

OUR REACTION OR IMPULSE FOR ACTION IS...

To seek the source

RELATED EMOTIONS

Serenity, ecstasy, peace, contentment

ITS PURPOSE IS TO...

Show us the source of our fulfillment

THE TIME ORIENTATION OF THIS EMOTION IS...

Present

HOW THIS EMOTION CAN GET IN THE WAY

Bliss puts us into a near narcotic state and may therefore disconnect us from taking action.

EMOTIONS WE CONFUSE IT WITH

Happiness means we feel fortunate or that things are turning out as we like. Bliss is something closer to serenity and peace or a strong sense of well-being.

HOW IT FEELS OR MOVES US

We go numb and allow ourselves to connect to the source of life.

HOW OUR BODY MIGHT FEEL

Relaxed and energized simultaneously

HOW OUR BREATH MIGHT BE

Slow, even, belly breathing

HOW OUR BODY MIGHT SHAPE ITSELF

Open, standing still

QUOTE

"Follow your bliss and the universe will open doors where there were only walls."—Joseph Campbell

BOLDNESS

ETYMOLOGICAL ROOT

Old English *beald* (West Saxon), *bald* (Anglian) "bold, brave, confident, strong"

WHAT WE THINK OR SAY

"I'm ready to act even though I feel fear."

ITS IMPACT ON OUR OPENNESS TO OTHERS

Opens us

OUR REACTION OR IMPULSE FOR ACTION IS...

Initiate action even when we are uncertain or fearful

RELATED EMOTIONS

Courage, confidence, zeal

ITS PURPOSE IS TO...

Allow us to act even when uncertain or scared

THE TIME ORIENTATION OF THIS EMOTION IS...

Future

HOW THIS EMOTION CAN GET IN THE WAY

"Fools rush in where angels fear to tread" sums up the danger of boldness when the risk being faced is ignored or denied.

EMOTIONS WE CONFUSE IT WITH

Courage is the capacity to act in the presence of fear, whereas boldness is to take action willingly.

HOW IT FEELS OR MOVES US

We step into action.

HOW OUR BODY MIGHT FEEL

Energized, tightness in the stomach

HOW OUR BREATH MIGHT BE

Elevated in the chest, fast-paced

HOW OUR BODY MIGHT SHAPE ITSELF

Moving towards, focused

QUOTE

"Whatever you can do, or dream you can do, begin it. Boldness has genius, power, and magic in it. Begin it now."—William Hutchinson Murray

BOREDOM

ETYMOLOGICAL ROOT

Old English *borian*, "to bore through, perforate"

WHAT WE THINK OR SAY

"There is nothing here of interest to me."

ITS IMPACT ON OUR OPENNESS TO OTHERS

Closes us

OUR REACTION OR IMPULSE FOR ACTION IS...

To look for something else to do, disengage

RELATED EMOTIONS

Ambivalence, uncertainty, resignation, indifference

ITS PURPOSE IS TO...

Move us away from things of little perceived value

THE TIME ORIENTATION OF THIS EMOTION IS...

Present

HOW THIS EMOTION CAN GET IN THE WAY

If we blame others for our boredom, we damage relationships and miss the opportunity of understanding what boredom is telling us.

EMOTIONS WE CONFUSE IT WITH

Rebelliousness. Boredom is telling us that we don't see anything of benefit in a certain activity, whereas rebelliousness is actively opposing the activity.

HOW IT FEELS OR MOVES US

We look for something that interests us more.

HOW OUR BODY MIGHT FEEL

Restless, low energy

HOW OUR BREATH MIGHT BE

Slow, shallow

HOW OUR BODY MIGHT SHAPE ITSELF

Collapsed, chest sunken, head down, eyes down

QUOTE

"When you pay attention to boredom, it gets unbelievably interesting."—Jon Kabat-Zinn

CALMNESS

ETYMOLOGICAL ROOT

From Late Latin *cauma*, "heat of the midday sun," a time when everything rests and is still, and from Greek *kauma*, "heat" (especially of the sun)

WHAT WE THINK OR SAY

"I feel peaceful."

ITS IMPACT ON OUR OPENNESS TO OTHERS

Opens us

- - - - - - - - - - - - - - - - - -   - - - - - - - - - - - - - - - - - - -

OUR REACTION OR IMPULSE FOR ACTION IS...

To be still

RELATED EMOTIONS

Acceptance, serenity, peace

- - - - - - - - - - - - - - - - - -   - - - - - - - - - - - - - - - - - - -

ITS PURPOSE IS TO...

Rest

THE TIME ORIENTATION OF THIS EMOTION IS...

Present

- -

HOW THIS EMOTION CAN GET IN THE WAY

Like acceptance, serenity, and peace, calmness is an oasis in the world of action. It allows us to rest, which is necessary, but from calmness we may not be well prepared to move into action.

EMOTIONS WE CONFUSE IT WITH

Acceptance. Calmness is largely a description of the feeling we are experiencing, whereas acceptance is the alignment of our belief with the way things are, thereby experiencing peace.

HOW IT FEELS OR MOVES US

To be quiet and still

HOW OUR BODY MIGHT FEEL

Relaxed and free of tension

HOW OUR BREATH MIGHT BE

Slow abdominal breathing

HOW OUR BODY MIGHT SHAPE ITSELF

Open, gaze is not focused

QUOTE

"Calm mind brings inner strength and self-confidence, so that's very important for good health."—Dalai Lama

CARE

ETYMOLOGICAL ROOT

Old English *carian*, *cearian*, "be anxious, grieve; to feel concern or interest"

WHAT WE THINK OR SAY

"It is important to me."

ITS IMPACT ON OUR OPENNESS TO OTHERS

Opens us

OUR REACTION OR IMPULSE FOR ACTION IS...

Attend to others or to a cause

RELATED EMOTIONS

Compassion, empathy, desire, affection

ITS PURPOSE IS TO...

Attend to others

THE TIME ORIENTATION OF THIS EMOTION IS...

Present

HOW THIS EMOTION CAN GET IN THE WAY

When we don't understand the difference between "caring about" and "caring for," we can believe that the former has less value than the latter. Both are important but have different functions. "Caring about" generates connection; "caring for" generates service to others.

EMOTIONS WE CONFUSE IT WITH

Service. Care comes in two forms—we can care about something/someone or we can care for it/them. Caring about someone does not implicitly mean we will take action, whereas caring for someone or being of service includes action by nature.

HOW IT FEELS OR MOVES US

Attend to others

HOW OUR BODY MIGHT FEEL

Relaxed, warm

HOW OUR BREATH MIGHT BE

Even-paced, low in the abdomen

HOW OUR BODY MIGHT SHAPE ITSELF

Open, moving towards, reaching towards

QUOTE

"Nobody cares how much you know, until they know how much you care."—Author unknown

CERTAINTY

ETYMOLOGICAL ROOT

From Latin *certus*, "sure, fixed, settled, determined"

WHAT WE THINK OR SAY

"I'm sure."

ITS IMPACT ON OUR OPENNESS TO OTHERS

Can close or open

OUR REACTION OR IMPULSE FOR ACTION IS...

To remain steadfast

RELATED EMOTIONS

Rectitude, arrogance, righteousness

ITS PURPOSE IS TO...

Act without hesitation

THE TIME ORIENTATION OF THIS EMOTION IS...

Present

HOW THIS EMOTION CAN GET IN THE WAY

One can be certain and wrong. It is not an uncommon experience for most of us. We believe something to be true to the degree that we defend it, only to find out we were misinformed or misunderstood. This has an impact on our public identity and relationships.

EMOTIONS WE CONFUSE IT WITH

Righteousness. Certainty means we do not have doubts, but does not mean we believe we have the only answer or are better than others. Righteousness means we believe we have the only legitimate answer and are morally correct.

HOW IT FEELS OR MOVES US

Unwavering

HOW OUR BODY MIGHT FEEL

Solid, grounded

HOW OUR BREATH MIGHT BE

Slow, even, medium deep

HOW OUR BODY MIGHT SHAPE ITSELF

Length, width, and depth balanced equally

QUOTE

"The demand for certainty is one which is natural to man, but is nevertheless an intellectual vice."—Bertrand Russell

COMPASSION

ETYMOLOGICAL ROOT

Latin *compassionem*, from *com-* "together" + *pati* "to suffer"

WHAT WE THINK OR SAY

"I'm with you in your challenges."

ITS IMPACT ON OUR OPENNESS TO OTHERS

Opens us

OUR REACTION OR IMPULSE FOR ACTION IS...

To be with another in his/her difficulty or pain

RELATED EMOTIONS

Sympathy, empathy, pity

ITS PURPOSE IS TO...

Be with others in their pain or struggle

THE TIME ORIENTATION OF THIS EMOTION IS...

Present

HOW THIS EMOTION CAN GET IN THE WAY

Compassion is a very helpful emotion for serving others in teaching, medicine, coaching, etc. However, it is not one we can substitute for empathy or sympathy when those are called for in the relationship.

EMOTIONS WE CONFUSE IT WITH

Empathy. Empathy is the re-creation, in ourselves, of the emotion of the other. Compassion allows us to maintain our own emotion while being fully present for the other.

HOW IT FEELS OR MOVES US

To be with others in their moments of difficulty

HOW OUR BODY MIGHT FEEL

Relaxed and energized simultaneously

HOW OUR BREATH MIGHT BE

Long, slow, and deep

HOW OUR BODY MIGHT SHAPE ITSELF

Open, moving towards

QUOTE

"If you want others to be happy, practice compassion. If you want to be happy, practice compassion."—Dalai Lama

CONFIDENCE

ETYMOLOGICAL ROOT

From Latin, assimilated form of *com* "with" + *fidere* "trust"

WHAT WE THINK OR SAY

"I believe it will happen."

ITS IMPACT ON OUR OPENNESS TO OTHERS

Opens us

OUR REACTION OR IMPULSE FOR ACTION IS...

To let go

RELATED EMOTIONS

Trust, arrogance, zeal, inspiration

ITS PURPOSE IS TO...

Allow us to put our attention on other things

THE TIME ORIENTATION OF THIS EMOTION IS...

Future

HOW THIS EMOTION CAN GET IN THE WAY

Confidence in excess means that we believe something will occur beyond what we have evidence for. So overconfidence is a kind of hope and is not grounded in competence.

EMOTIONS WE CONFUSE IT WITH

Arrogance. Confidence is the trust that a thing will happen or that we can do it successfully. It is not comparative to others, whereas arrogance is the belief that we are superior.

HOW IT FEELS OR MOVES US

We feel safe and assured

HOW OUR BODY MIGHT FEEL

Steady, with a calm, focused energy

HOW OUR BREATH MIGHT BE

Steady, even, paced

HOW OUR BODY MIGHT SHAPE ITSELF

Length, width, and depth equally balanced and full

QUOTE

"Be courteous to all, but intimate with few, and let those few be well tried before you give them your confidence."
—George Washington

71

CONFUSION

The emotion is.......

ETYMOLOGICAL ROOT

From Latin *confusionem*, "a mingling, mixing, blending, disorder," and *confundere* "to pour together"

WHAT WE THINK OR SAY

"This doesn't fit into my understanding."

ITS IMPACT ON OUR OPENNESS TO OTHERS

Closes us

OUR REACTION OR IMPULSE FOR ACTION IS...

Try to figure out how a new idea fits into our worldview

RELATED EMOTIONS

Doubt, uncertainty, ambivalence

ITS PURPOSE IS TO...

Make sense of things that aren't part of our current understanding

THE TIME ORIENTATION OF THIS EMOTION IS...

Present

HOW THIS EMOTION CAN GET IN THE WAY

Confusion can trigger anxiety or fear. When this occurs, we will avoid it rather than utilize it to explore new possibilities

EMOTIONS WE CONFUSE IT WITH

Skepticism is the emotion we experience when we are trying to decide whether to maintain our previous belief or to change our belief to a new one we are being presented.

HOW IT FEELS OR MOVES US

To figure it out

HOW OUR BODY MIGHT FEEL

Like it wants to move

HOW OUR BREATH MIGHT BE

Shallow in the chest, faster-paced than at rest

HOW OUR BODY MIGHT SHAPE ITSELF

Head down to one side, forehead wrinkled, shoulders moving in towards the sternum

QUOTE

"Confusion is a word we have invented for an order which is not understood."—Henry Miller

CONTEMPT

ETYMOLOGICAL ROOT

Latin from past participle of *contemnere*, "to scorn, despise"

WHAT WE THINK OR SAY

"You'll never amount to anything; you're unworthy."

OUR REACTION OR IMPULSE FOR ACTION IS...

Condescend or treat others without respect

ITS PURPOSE IS TO...

Know our standard relative to respecting others

ITS IMPACT ON OUR OPENNESS TO OTHERS

Closes us

RELATED EMOTIONS

Disrespect, revulsion, cynicism, dislike, distaste

THE TIME ORIENTATION OF THIS EMOTION IS...

Present

HOW THIS EMOTION CAN GET IN THE WAY

Contempt tends to show up with some level of arrogance, and both dismiss others as "less than." Neither is grounds for a generative relationship.

EMOTIONS WE CONFUSE IT WITH

Hate. In hate we want to avoid a thing or person at all costs. In contempt we are still connected with the thing or person, but disparaging it/them.

HOW IT FEELS OR MOVES US

To treat others as less important than we believe we are.

HOW OUR BODY MIGHT FEEL

Tight in the chest and upper back

HOW OUR BREATH MIGHT BE

Shallow, faster than resting pace

HOW OUR BODY MIGHT SHAPE ITSELF

Nose in the air, chin lifted, moving away

QUOTE

"Preservation of one's own culture does not require contempt or disrespect for other cultures."—Cesar Chavez

CONTENTMENT

ETYMOLOGICAL ROOT

From Latin *contentus*, "contained, satisfied"

WHAT WE THINK OR SAY

"I'm satisfied."

ITS IMPACT ON OUR OPENNESS TO OTHERS

Opens us

OUR REACTION OR IMPULSE FOR ACTION IS…

To rest and enjoy

RELATED EMOTIONS

Satisfaction, serenity, peace

ITS PURPOSE IS TO…

Let us know when we have done enough

THE TIME ORIENTATION OF THIS EMOTION IS…

Present

HOW THIS EMOTION CAN GET IN THE WAY

Contentment lives alongside peace and satisfaction and is restful. However, it is not an emotion from which we can act or defend ourselves easily.

EMOTIONS WE CONFUSE IT WITH

Satisfaction. Contentment means that I do not feel the need to change anything about my circumstances, whereas satisfaction is the belief that "I have enough." Neither moves me to get more, but for different reasons.

HOW IT FEELS OR MOVES US

We let go of trying to improve or change things.

HOW OUR BODY MIGHT FEEL

Relaxed and at peace

HOW OUR BREATH MIGHT BE

Slow, even, medium depth

HOW OUR BODY MIGHT SHAPE ITSELF

Tendency to move back and down

QUOTE

"Health is the greatest gift, contentment the greatest wealth, faithfulness the best relationship."—Buddha

COURAGE

ETYMOLOGICAL ROOT

From Latin *cor*, "with heart," as the seat of emotions

WHAT WE THINK OR SAY

"I can do it even though I'm afraid."

ITS IMPACT ON OUR OPENNESS TO OTHERS

Opens us

OUR REACTION OR IMPULSE FOR ACTION IS...

To be able to act in the presence of fear

RELATED EMOTIONS

Boldness, confidence, trust

ITS PURPOSE IS TO...

Give us the possibility to act in the presence of fear

THE TIME ORIENTATION OF THIS EMOTION IS...

Future

HOW THIS EMOTION CAN GET IN THE WAY

Blind courage or courage that does not account for the risk we are taking can put us in precarious situations.

EMOTIONS WE CONFUSE IT WITH

Boldness. Courage is the ability to act in the face of fear, whereas boldness is stepping into the act when in fear.

HOW IT FEELS OR MOVES US

To do things we are scared to do

HOW OUR BODY MIGHT FEEL

Energized, streaming energy flowing up and down the body

HOW OUR BREATH MIGHT BE

Fast, in the upper chest

HOW OUR BODY MIGHT SHAPE ITSELF

Moving towards, erect, full length, eyes focused on the object of fear

QUOTE

"I learned that courage was not the absence of fear, but the triumph over it. The brave man is not he who does not feel afraid, but he who conquers that fear."—Nelson Mandela

COVETOUSNESS

ETYMOLOGICAL ROOT

From Latin *cupiditas*, "Passionate desire, eagerness, ambition, longing for"

WHAT WE THINK OR SAY

"I want it."

ITS IMPACT ON OUR OPENNESS TO OTHERS

Closes us

OUR REACTION OR IMPULSE FOR ACTION IS...

To take

RELATED EMOTIONS

Desire, envy, jealousy

ITS PURPOSE IS TO...

Get things we want

THE TIME ORIENTATION OF THIS EMOTION IS...

Present

HOW THIS EMOTION CAN GET IN THE WAY

We may put more attention on what we would like to take away from someone than the relationship with them.

EMOTIONS WE CONFUSE IT WITH

Envy. Many people believe that envy means we want to take the thing we desire away from its owner, but that is covetousness.

HOW IT FEELS OR MOVES US

To look for ways to take what is not rightfully ours

HOW OUR BODY MIGHT FEEL

Ungrounded

HOW OUR BREATH MIGHT BE

High in the chest, medium-paced

HOW OUR BODY MIGHT SHAPE ITSELF

Leaning towards what you are wanting, up and forward

QUOTE

"Desire of having is the sin of covetousness."
—William Shakespeare

CURIOSITY

ETYMOLOGICAL ROOT

From Latin *curiositatem*, "desire of knowledge, inquisitiveness"

WHAT WE THINK OR SAY

"Tell me more."

ITS IMPACT ON OUR OPENNESS TO OTHERS

Opens us

OUR REACTION OR IMPULSE FOR ACTION IS...

Look for more information

RELATED EMOTIONS

Intrigue, fascination, wonder

ITS PURPOSE IS TO...

Keep us learning, engaged in life, and looking for new possibilities

THE TIME ORIENTATION OF THIS EMOTION IS...

Future

HOW THIS EMOTION CAN GET IN THE WAY

"Curiosity killed the cat." Furthermore, someone who is constantly curious becomes boring or irritating to others with their relentless questioning.

EMOTIONS WE CONFUSE IT WITH

Skepticism. Skepticism means I'm trying to decide whether to believe what I always have or some new idea. Curiosity is the exploration of all ideas, but does not include making a choice about what to believe.

HOW IT FEELS OR MOVES US

Energy forward, moves us to ask questions or search for new information

HOW OUR BODY MIGHT FEEL

Energized, alert, focused

HOW OUR BREATH MIGHT BE

Slightly faster than resting, but even and relaxed

HOW OUR BODY MIGHT SHAPE ITSELF

Open, chest full in the front and back, slight bend forward

QUOTE

"Curiosity is the wick in the candle of learning."
—*William Arthur Ward*

CYNICISM

ETYMOLOGICAL ROOT

From Greek *kynikos*, "a follower of Antisthenes," literally "dog-like," from *kyon*, "dog"

WHAT WE THINK OR SAY

"I distrust others' apparent good intentions."

ITS IMPACT ON OUR OPENNESS TO OTHERS

Closes us

OUR REACTION OR IMPULSE FOR ACTION IS…

To reject all possibilities and recruit others to your view

RELATED EMOTIONS

Resignation, doubt, skepticism

ITS PURPOSE IS TO…

Let us challenge ungrounded excitement

THE TIME ORIENTATION OF THIS EMOTION IS…

Past or present

HOW THIS EMOTION CAN GET IN THE WAY

In organizations the most caustic emotion is cynicism. It means that we are resigned and we want to convince others to join us. Cynicism gives the person experiencing it power and is difficult to change because of that.

EMOTIONS WE CONFUSE IT WITH

Resentment means we believe something is unfair, whereas in cynicism we question or dismiss others' intentions no matter how good.

HOW IT FEELS OR MOVES US

To dismiss or ridicule others' ideas

HOW OUR BODY MIGHT FEEL

Tight in the chest, heavy

HOW OUR BREATH MIGHT BE

Shallow, faster than resting

HOW OUR BODY MIGHT SHAPE ITSELF

Moving downwards and away, head tilted to the side and down, shoulders slightly elevated

QUOTE

"A cynic is a man who knows the price of everything and the value of nothing."—Oscar Wilde

DELIGHT

ETYMOLOGICAL ROOT

From Latin *delectare*, "to allure, delight, charm, please," and *delicere*, "entice"

WHAT WE THINK OR SAY

"I'm very happy."

ITS IMPACT ON OUR OPENNESS TO OTHERS

Opens us

OUR REACTION OR IMPULSE FOR ACTION IS…

To enjoy and usually comment on the experience

RELATED EMOTIONS

Hilarity, joy, happiness

ITS PURPOSE IS TO…

Show us what pleases us

THE TIME ORIENTATION OF THIS EMOTION IS…

Present

HOW THIS EMOTION CAN GET IN THE WAY

Just because we are delighted, it doesn't mean that the experience was positive or enjoyable for others, which means we can delight in the pain or suffering of others.

EMOTIONS WE CONFUSE IT WITH

Joy. Joy means we believe life is worth celebrating; delight, that we are pleased or charmed with an experience.

HOW IT FEELS OR MOVES US

To enjoy the moment

HOW OUR BODY MIGHT FEEL

Light, moving upwards and forward, stand towards

HOW OUR BREATH MIGHT BE

Long, slow deep breaths

HOW OUR BODY MIGHT SHAPE ITSELF

Full length, smile, head uplifted slightly, fully erect

QUOTE

"And forget not that the earth delights to feel your bare feet and the winds long to play with your hair."
—Khalil Gibran

DENIAL

The emotion is................

ETYMOLOGICAL ROOT

From Latin *denegare*, "to deny, reject, refuse"

WHAT WE THINK OR SAY

"If I don't pay attention, it will go away."

ITS IMPACT ON OUR OPENNESS TO OTHERS

Closes us

OUR REACTION OR IMPULSE FOR ACTION IS...

To refuse to look

RELATED EMOTIONS

Naïveté, confusion, distaste

ITS PURPOSE IS TO...

Allow us to move ahead when knowing the reality of the situation might immobilize us

THE TIME ORIENTATION OF THIS EMOTION IS...

Past

HOW THIS EMOTION CAN GET IN THE WAY

Denial can get in our way, because its nature is to look away or disregard what we see. From denial, we cannot look at or engage with reality. We live in a fantasy.

EMOTIONS WE CONFUSE IT WITH

Naïveté. Denial is a refusal to believe something we see, whereas naïveté is the inability to believe something is evil or bad.

HOW IT FEELS OR MOVES US

To ignore

HOW OUR BODY MIGHT FEEL

Rooted, tight

HOW OUR BREATH MIGHT BE

High in the chest, shallow, quick

HOW OUR BODY MIGHT SHAPE ITSELF

Head tilted down, width diminished

QUOTE

"Denial helps us to pace our feelings of grief. There is a grace in denial. It is nature's way of letting in only as much as we can handle."—Elisabeth Kübler-Ross

DESIRE

ETYMOLOGICAL ROOT

Latin *desiderare*, "long for, wish for; demand, expect," original sense perhaps "await what the stars will bring," from the phrase *de sidere*, "from the stars"

WHAT WE THINK OR SAY

"I want."

ITS IMPACT ON OUR OPENNESS TO OTHERS

Opens us

OUR REACTION OR IMPULSE FOR ACTION IS...

To seek out what we are longing for

RELATED EMOTIONS

Passion, love, zeal, adoration

ITS PURPOSE IS TO...

Know what we want

THE TIME ORIENTATION OF THIS EMOTION IS...

Present

HOW THIS EMOTION CAN GET IN THE WAY

Desire causes us to move toward or try to be close to another. As long as the desire is shared by the other, we are acting in accord. However, desire can prompt us to move closer to others who do not want the same relationship.

EMOTIONS WE CONFUSE IT WITH

Lust. Desire literally means to "wait for what the stars are bringing" and thus has an unearthly origin; lust refers to an appetite or sensuous pleasure and thus is very much earthbound.

HOW IT FEELS OR MOVES US

To pursue what we want

HOW OUR BODY MIGHT FEEL

Warm, energized

HOW OUR BREATH MIGHT BE

Mid-chest, slightly elevated from resting rate, depending on the level of desire

HOW OUR BODY MIGHT SHAPE ITSELF

Moving towards, open chest and arms

QUOTE

"Everyone has been made for some particular work, and the desire for that work has been put in every heart."
—*Rumi*

DESPAIR

The emotion is...............

ETYMOLOGICAL ROOT

From Latin *desperare*, "to despair, to lose all hope," from *de-* "without" + *sperare* "to hope"

WHAT WE THINK OR SAY

"I have no hope; I see no possibilities."

ITS IMPACT ON OUR OPENNESS TO OTHERS

Closes us

OUR REACTION OR IMPULSE FOR ACTION IS...

To give up

RELATED EMOTIONS

Resignation, sadness, hopelessness

ITS PURPOSE IS TO...

Allow us to submit

THE TIME ORIENTATION OF THIS EMOTION IS...

Present, future

HOW THIS EMOTION CAN GET IN THE WAY

In despair we don't see the possibility of a better future. In fact, we may not be able to imagine a future at all. At this level, despair can lead to giving up on life, because if we cannot imagine a future, we have nothing to "live into."

EMOTIONS WE CONFUSE IT WITH

Sadness. Despair is similar to hopelessness and means to give up, whereas sadness is the recognition that we've lost something/somebody we care about and thus points to what is important to us.

HOW IT FEELS OR MOVES US

To give up or surrender

HOW OUR BODY MIGHT FEEL

Heavy

HOW OUR BREATH MIGHT BE

Deep long staccato exhales

HOW OUR BODY MIGHT SHAPE ITSELF

Chest and shoulders concave, direction of the body is down

QUOTE

"Only a man who has felt ultimate despair is capable of feeling ultimate bliss."—Alexandre Dumas

DIGNITY

ETYMOLOGICAL ROOT

From Latin *dignitatem*, "worthiness," and *dignus*, "worth, worthy, proper, fitting"

WHAT WE THINK OR SAY

"I am worthy; I decide."

ITS IMPACT ON OUR OPENNESS TO OTHERS

Neutral to open

OUR REACTION OR IMPULSE FOR ACTION IS...

To act as a legitimate human being deserving of respect

RELATED EMOTIONS

Respect, honor

ITS PURPOSE IS TO...

Set and protect personal boundaries

THE TIME ORIENTATION OF THIS EMOTION IS...

Present

HOW THIS EMOTION CAN GET IN THE WAY

Dignity can get in the way if we use it as a weapon or tool to manipulate. If we set false boundaries to trick or cause problems for others, we are not using dignity as it was intended.

EMOTIONS WE CONFUSE IT WITH

Pride. Dignity means "we set the boundaries of how we will allow ourselves to be treated," whereas pride means we believe we've done a good thing and want others to know.

HOW IT FEELS OR MOVES US

To take a stand for ourselves

HOW OUR BODY MIGHT FEEL

Relaxed and alert

HOW OUR BREATH MIGHT BE

Long, slow, even, deep

HOW OUR BODY MIGHT SHAPE ITSELF

Erect but not rigid, maximum length and width

QUOTE

"Any man or institution that tries to rob me of my dignity will lose."—Nelson Mandela

DISAPPOINTMENT

ETYMOLOGICAL ROOT

From Middle French *desappointer* (14c.), "undo the appointment, remove from office," from *des-* + *appointer* "appoint"

WHAT WE THINK OR SAY

"This isn't what I expected."

ITS IMPACT ON OUR OPENNESS TO OTHERS

Closes us

OUR REACTION OR IMPULSE FOR ACTION IS…

To look for the disconnect

RELATED EMOTIONS

Dismay, surprise, sadness

ITS PURPOSE IS TO…

Align our expectations with reality

THE TIME ORIENTATION OF THIS EMOTION IS…

Past

HOW THIS EMOTION CAN GET IN THE WAY

Disappointment is often interpreted as meaning there is "something wrong," and from there we look for someone other than us to blame. If there is someone responsible, it is usually us, because disappointment results from our expectations being misaligned with reality.

EMOTIONS WE CONFUSE IT WITH

Resignation. Disappointment means that something we looked forward to is not going to happen as we thought. Resignation is the belief that nothing we do will make any difference.

HOW IT FEELS OR MOVES US

To confirm reality and change our expectations

HOW OUR BODY MIGHT FEEL

Sluggish, slow

HOW OUR BREATH MIGHT BE

Sighs or deep sighs, depending on the depth of the disappointment

HOW OUR BODY MIGHT SHAPE ITSELF

Shoulders dropped, chest slightly concave

QUOTE

"Landscape photography is the supreme test of the photographer—and often the supreme disappointment."
—Ansel Adams

DISDAIN

ETYMOLOGICAL ROOT

From Old French *desdeignier*, from "do the opposite" + "treat as worthy"

WHAT WE THINK OR SAY

"You're not worth my time."

ITS IMPACT ON OUR OPENNESS TO OTHERS

Closes us

OUR REACTION OR IMPULSE FOR ACTION IS...

To dismiss or disrespect

RELATED EMOTIONS

Contempt, disrespect, disgust

ITS PURPOSE IS TO...

Shows us who we believe is worthy

THE TIME ORIENTATION OF THIS EMOTION IS...

Present

HOW THIS EMOTION CAN GET IN THE WAY

When we treat someone with disdain, we are labeling them as unworthy, meaning they do not have value to us. This makes any generative relationship impossible.

EMOTIONS WE CONFUSE IT WITH

Contempt means to despise someone, whereas disdain is to treat them as if they are unworthy. Contempt is closer to hate and disdain closer to disrespect.

HOW IT FEELS OR MOVES US

To disregard others or see them as unimportant

HOW OUR BODY MIGHT FEEL

Heavy

HOW OUR BREATH MIGHT BE

Shallow, even

HOW OUR BODY MIGHT SHAPE ITSELF

Length and width diminished, head down

QUOTE

"Towering genius disdains a beaten path. It seeks regions hitherto unexplored."—Abraham Lincoln

DISGUST

ETYMOLOGICAL ROOT

Latin from *des-*, "opposite of" + *gustare*, "to taste"

WHAT WE THINK OR SAY

"This experience leaves a bad taste in my mouth."

ITS IMPACT ON OUR OPENNESS TO OTHERS

Closes us

OUR REACTION OR IMPULSE FOR ACTION IS...

To reject, turn away or not participate

RELATED EMOTIONS

Revulsion, scorn, dislike

ITS PURPOSE IS TO...

Help us persevere and act in accordance with our values and beliefs by rejecting things we find distasteful

THE TIME ORIENTATION OF THIS EMOTION IS...

Present

100

HOW THIS EMOTION CAN GET IN THE WAY

We may judge something we find disgusting as wrong or bad when in fact it just doesn't align with what we find to be in good taste.

EMOTIONS WE CONFUSE IT WITH

Revulsion. Disgust literally means to "taste bad" and is the feeling we can have with a situation or person, and because of that we may want to avoid them, whereas revulsion makes us want to "tear away" from a person or situation and is much more profound.

HOW IT FEELS OR MOVES US

Literally makes us want to spit out or eliminate "the taste" of the experience

HOW OUR BODY MIGHT FEEL

Tightened, with a queasy stomach

HOW OUR BREATH MIGHT BE

Short, shallow, fast, in the upper chest

HOW OUR BODY MIGHT SHAPE ITSELF

Turning away, closing, mouth turned down

QUOTE

"The greatest pleasures are only narrowly separated from disgust."—Marcus Tullius Cicero

DISLIKE

ETYMOLOGICAL ROOT

From Latin *dis-*, "apart, in a different direction, between," +
Middle English shortening of Old English *gelic*, "like, similar"

WHAT WE THINK OR SAY

"I don't want this."

ITS IMPACT ON OUR OPENNESS TO OTHERS

Closes us

OUR REACTION OR IMPULSE FOR ACTION IS...

To avoid being with or near
someone or something

RELATED EMOTIONS

Hate, disgust, distaste, revulsion

ITS PURPOSE IS TO...

Tell us what we don't want

THE TIME ORIENTATION OF THIS EMOTION IS...

Present

HOW THIS EMOTION CAN GET IN THE WAY

At times we can equate disliking something with it being bad or wrong. When we do this, we lose the possibility of nonjudgmentally investigating what it is about the thing or person that has us wanting to move away or avoid it.

EMOTIONS WE CONFUSE IT WITH

Hate. Dislike means we don't enjoy the company of another person or a situation, whereas hate is to have a "passionate aversion" to a person or situation.

HOW IT FEELS OR MOVES US

Stay away

HOW OUR BODY MIGHT FEEL

Teeth clenched, jaw tight, stomach in a knot

HOW OUR BREATH MIGHT BE

Shallow, rapid, depending on how severe the dislike

HOW OUR BODY MIGHT SHAPE ITSELF

Turning away from, closed

QUOTE

"He has all of the virtues I dislike and none of the vices I admire."—*Winston Churchill*

103

DISMAY

The emotion is.................

ETYMOLOGICAL ROOT

From Latin *de-* + *exmagare,* "divest of power or ability"

WHAT WE THINK OR SAY

"I thought I'd be able to."

ITS IMPACT ON OUR OPENNESS TO OTHERS

Closes us

OUR REACTION OR IMPULSE FOR ACTION IS...

Go along with what is happening

RELATED EMOTIONS

Disappointment, surprise

ITS PURPOSE IS TO...

Help us recognize the limits of our influence

THE TIME ORIENTATION OF THIS EMOTION IS...

Past

HOW THIS EMOTION CAN GET IN THE WAY

Dismay is somewhat similar to disappointment. When we feel dismay, we may choose to fight against it and attempt to influence or exercise power we do not have. That can put us in danger or cause breakdowns in relationships.

EMOTIONS WE CONFUSE IT WITH

Disappointment. Dismay is a mild surprise that I didn't have the power to do what I thought I could, whereas disappointment is a strong surprise because things didn't go as I expected.

HOW IT FEELS OR MOVES US

Wonder about our level of power or influence

HOW OUR BODY MIGHT FEEL

Tense

HOW OUR BREATH MIGHT BE

Deep, slow exhales, short inhales

HOW OUR BODY MIGHT SHAPE ITSELF

Shortened width and length

QUOTE

"I was drawn to it, much to my father's dismay. He wanted me to be a pianist like he was, but I had coarser tastes— like that old joke: What do you call a guy who hangs around with musicians? A drummer."—Miguel Ferrer

DISPASSION

ETYMOLOGICAL ROOT

Directly from Latin *dis-*, "apart, in a different direction, between," + Greek *pathos*, literally "suffering," from *polian* "to endure"

WHAT WE THINK OR SAY

"I understand the situation but am not caught up in the emotion of it."

ITS IMPACT ON OUR OPENNESS TO OTHERS

Opens us

OUR REACTION OR IMPULSE FOR ACTION IS...

To consider from a balanced perspective

RELATED EMOTIONS

Equanimity, calmness, apathy

ITS PURPOSE IS TO...

Allow us to observe our emotions from a viewpoint outside ourselves

THE TIME ORIENTATION OF THIS EMOTION IS...

Present

HOW THIS EMOTION CAN GET IN THE WAY

Dispassion is "to be apart from our emotions." We are not exactly being objective, but we are not connected with and including emotions in a central way in our conversations and decisions. This can lead us to miss the benefits of empathy and compassion.

EMOTIONS WE CONFUSE IT WITH

Equanimity. In dispassion we are separated from emotions or not feeling their influence, whereas equanimity occurs when we balance all perspectives.

HOW IT FEELS OR MOVES US

Stay balanced

HOW OUR BODY MIGHT FEEL

Relaxed and grounded

HOW OUR BREATH MIGHT BE

Evenness of breath, diaphragmatic

HOW OUR BODY MIGHT SHAPE ITSELF

Length, width, and depth are balanced

QUOTE

"Dispassion is the best of mental states...."
—*Gautama Buddha*

DISSATISFACTION

WHAT WE THINK OR SAY

"I don't have enough; something is missing."

ITS IMPACT ON OUR OPENNESS TO OTHERS

Closes us

OUR REACTION OR IMPULSE FOR ACTION IS...

To seek more of what we lack

RELATED EMOTIONS

Dismay, disappointment

ITS PURPOSE IS TO...

Tell us what we believe we lack

THE TIME ORIENTATION OF THIS EMOTION IS...

Present

HOW THIS EMOTION CAN GET IN THE WAY

Dissatisfaction tells us we believe something is missing for us. It does not mean anything is wrong, but is an assessment that something is "not enough." If we only focus on this rather than balancing it with satisfaction, we will fail to notice the "good things" we already have.

EMOTIONS WE CONFUSE IT WITH

Disappointment. Dissatisfaction is the belief that we are lacking something to have a complete life. It is not that we expected what we are missing or it was promised to us as in disappointment, but only that we see a possibility.

HOW IT FEELS OR MOVES US

To get more of what we believe is missing

HOW OUR BODY MIGHT FEEL

Tense, tightness in chest and/or belly

HOW OUR BREATH MIGHT BE

Short, shallow

HOW OUR BODY MIGHT SHAPE ITSELF

Shoulders slumped, chest concave, length is shortened

QUOTE

"A dog owns nothing, yet is seldom dissatisfied."
—*Proverb*

DOUBT

ETYMOLOGICAL ROOT

Rooted in the Latin *dubiosus*, which meant "vacillating, fluctuating, or wavering"

WHAT WE THINK OR SAY

"I'm unsure because I never did this before."

ITS IMPACT ON OUR OPENNESS TO OTHERS

Closes us

OUR REACTION OR IMPULSE FOR ACTION IS...

To question what I'm doing and how I'm doing it

RELATED EMOTIONS

Anxiety, fear, uncertainty, confusion, ambivalence

ITS PURPOSE IS TO...

Focus our attention on preparation for something new

THE TIME ORIENTATION OF THIS EMOTION IS...

Future

HOW THIS EMOTION CAN GET IN THE WAY

Doubt causes us to hesitate. Although this is important in many situations, as it allows us to reflect, gather more information, and choose, it is a hindrance when there is no more information to get or more information will not help us be sure what choice to make.

EMOTIONS WE CONFUSE IT WITH

Anxiety. Doubt means "I'm unsure because this is new." Anxiety is the belief that something may hurt me. Anxiety does not occur only in new contexts, whereas doubt does.

HOW IT FEELS OR MOVES US

To double-check our preparations

HOW OUR BODY MIGHT FEEL

A little tense in the forehead

HOW OUR BREATH MIGHT BE

Slow and shallow

HOW OUR BODY MIGHT SHAPE ITSELF

Shortened length, chest slightly concave

QUOTE

"Doubt is not a pleasant condition, but certainty is absurd."—Voltaire

DREAD

ETYMOLOGICAL ROOT

Late 12c., a shortening of Old English *adrædan*, "counsel or advise against"

WHAT WE THINK OR SAY

"I can't face this."

ITS IMPACT ON OUR OPENNESS TO OTHERS

Closes us

OUR REACTION OR IMPULSE FOR ACTION IS...

To avoid if possible or proceed with utmost caution

RELATED EMOTIONS

Fear, anxiety, terror

ITS PURPOSE IS TO...

Avoid what we fear

THE TIME ORIENTATION OF THIS EMOTION IS...

Future

HOW THIS EMOTION CAN GET IN THE WAY

Dread keeps us from "opening the lid." It can keep us safe from unknown or subversive danger, but it can also cut us off from all experiences because we want to avoid all possibilities of danger.

EMOTIONS WE CONFUSE IT WITH

Fear. Fear is the belief that something specific may harm me in a given situation, whereas dread occurs when we are doing something that may be unavoidable but scary.

HOW IT FEELS OR MOVES US

To avoid if at all possible

HOW OUR BODY MIGHT FEEL

Heavy, tired

HOW OUR BREATH MIGHT BE

Long and slow; exhale longer than the inhale

HOW OUR BODY MIGHT SHAPE ITSELF

Head down, chest concave, length is shortened

QUOTE

"The dread of evil is a much more forcible principle of human actions than the prospect of good."—John Locke

EASE

The emotion is..................................

ETYMOLOGICAL ROOT

From Old French *aise*, "comfort, pleasure, well-being, opportunity"

WHAT WE THINK OR SAY

"I feel relaxed and no tension at all."

ITS IMPACT ON OUR OPENNESS TO OTHERS

Opens us

OUR REACTION OR IMPULSE FOR ACTION IS...

To enjoy the moment without tension

RELATED EMOTIONS

Serenity, peace, contentment

ITS PURPOSE IS TO...

Show us where we are competent or safe

THE TIME ORIENTATION OF THIS EMOTION IS...

Present

HOW THIS EMOTION CAN GET IN THE WAY

Ease is the emotion of contentment, well-being, and peace. It is restful but, like other restful emotions, is not an emotion we can act or defend ourselves from.

EMOTIONS WE CONFUSE IT WITH

Contentment. Ease is comfort due to a sense of well-being, whereas contentment is the feeling that I don't need to change anything for life to be good.

HOW IT FEELS OR MOVES US

To relax and enjoy

HOW OUR BODY MIGHT FEEL

Relaxed, tendency to move back and down, flowing energy moving through the body

HOW OUR BREATH MIGHT BE

Slow chest breathing

HOW OUR BODY MIGHT SHAPE ITSELF

Open, head up, chin up, flow

QUOTE

"Try to be like the turtle—at ease in your own shell."
—*Bill Copeland*

ECSTASY

ETYMOLOGICAL ROOT

"Mystically absorbed," from Greek *ekstatikos*, "unstable, inclined to depart from"

WHAT WE THINK OR SAY

"This is an incomprehensible, mystical feeling."

ITS IMPACT ON OUR OPENNESS TO OTHERS

Opens us

OUR REACTION OR IMPULSE FOR ACTION IS...

To flow with the experience

RELATED EMOTIONS

Lust, passion, elation, euphoria, bliss

ITS PURPOSE IS TO...

Show us the enormity and incomprehensibility of the universe

THE TIME ORIENTATION OF THIS EMOTION IS...

Present

HOW THIS EMOTION CAN GET IN THE WAY

In true ecstasy we "depart from this realm." In ecstasy we are not aware of what is occurring in "this realm" and may act in ways that are dangerous or cause harm to others.

EMOTIONS WE CONFUSE IT WITH

Passion. Ecstasy means to be "mystically absorbed," and passion is a deep yearning to meld with something or someone.

HOW IT FEELS OR MOVES US

To soar

HOW OUR BODY MIGHT FEEL

Alive, energized, pulsating energy flowing through

HOW OUR BREATH MIGHT BE

Deep, slow, full breaths, inhale longer and more full than exhale

HOW OUR BODY MIGHT SHAPE ITSELF

Jumping up and down, crying, yelling, arms fully extended above you, head up, wide smile, eyes bright. Full length, width, and depth.

QUOTE

"Only the united beat of sex and heart together can create ecstasy."—Anaïs Nin, Delta of Venus

ELATION

The emotion is..............

ETYMOLOGICAL ROOT

Latin *elationem*, "a carrying out, a lifting up"

WHAT WE THINK OR SAY

"I feel I'm being carried away."

ITS IMPACT ON OUR OPENNESS TO OTHERS

Opens us

OUR REACTION OR IMPULSE FOR ACTION IS...

To enjoy, share, and celebrate

RELATED EMOTIONS

Ecstasy, euphoria, excitement, ebullience, exhilaration

ITS PURPOSE IS TO...

Allow us to celebrate unusual good fortune or accomplishment

THE TIME ORIENTATION OF THIS EMOTION IS...

Present

HOW THIS EMOTION CAN GET IN THE WAY

Elation, like euphoria, enchantment, ecstasy, and other emotions takes us out of day-to-day experiences and challenges. They are emotions we need, but also want to be sure don't become habits as a way to avoid unpleasant parts of life.

EMOTIONS WE CONFUSE IT WITH

Exuberance. Elation is "a lifting up," whereas exuberance is an "overabundance." Both can be good things, but they refer to different experiences.

HOW IT FEELS OR MOVES US	HOW OUR BODY MIGHT FEEL
To shout	Light, energized

HOW OUR BREATH MIGHT BE	HOW OUR BODY MIGHT SHAPE ITSELF
Fast, mid-chest breathing	Tendency to move up and forward, head up, big smile with open mouth

QUOTE

"Real elation is when you feel you could touch a star without standing on tiptoe."—Doug Larson

EMBARRASSMENT

WHAT WE THINK OR SAY

"I'd rather other people not know what I did."

ITS IMPACT ON OUR OPENNESS TO OTHERS

Closes us

OUR REACTION OR IMPULSE FOR ACTION IS...

To hide what we have done

RELATED EMOTIONS

Shame, shyness, mortification

ITS PURPOSE IS TO...

Maintain our public identity

THE TIME ORIENTATION OF THIS EMOTION IS...

Past or present

HOW THIS EMOTION CAN GET IN THE WAY

In embarrassment we want to hide things we've done from others. We do this in an attempt to protect our public identity or to influence how others see us.

EMOTIONS WE CONFUSE IT WITH

Shame is the experience of having "broken the norms or rules of a community we are part of." Embarrassment is wanting to avoid others seeing us commit an error or do something awkwardly.

HOW IT FEELS OR MOVES US

To hide what we've done

HOW OUR BODY MIGHT FEEL

Flushed, warm

HOW OUR BREATH MIGHT BE

Light, shallow

HOW OUR BODY MIGHT SHAPE ITSELF

Tendency to turn away, head down, chest concave

QUOTE

"Remembering that I'll be dead soon is the most important tool I've ever encountered to help me make the big choices in life. Because almost everything—all external expectations, all pride, all fear of embarrassment or failure—these things just fall away in the face of death, leaving only what is truly important."—Steve Jobs

EMPATHY

The emotion is..............

ETYMOLOGICAL ROOT

Greek *empatheia*, "passion, state of emotion"

WHAT WE THINK OR SAY

"I am feeling what you are feeling."

ITS IMPACT ON OUR OPENNESS TO OTHERS

Opens us

OUR REACTION OR IMPULSE FOR ACTION IS...

To share emotions with another

RELATED EMOTIONS

Sympathy, compassion, pity, care

ITS PURPOSE IS TO...

Allow us to feel what others are feeling

THE TIME ORIENTATION OF THIS EMOTION IS...

Present

HOW THIS EMOTION CAN GET IN THE WAY

Empathy allows me to share the emotion of the other person to genuinely understand their experience. However, since we are in the same emotion they are, we will see the world as they do. From there it will be impossible to help them shift to a new story of their experience if they wish to.

EMOTIONS WE CONFUSE IT WITH

Compassion. Empathy means joining someone in the emotion they are in and thus seeing the world as they do. Compassion is maintaining your own emotion and perspective while being present for the other. They are different ways of being with others.

HOW IT FEELS OR MOVES US

To feel what the other person is feeling

HOW OUR BODY MIGHT FEEL

Relaxed, at ease

HOW OUR BREATH MIGHT BE

Slow, even, diaphragmatic

HOW OUR BODY MIGHT SHAPE ITSELF

Open, tendency to move towards

QUOTE

"There is zero correlation between IQ and emotional empathy... They're controlled by different parts of the brain."—Daniel Goleman

ENCHANTMENT

ETYMOLOGICAL ROOT

From Latin *incantare*, "to fix a spell upon"

WHAT WE THINK OR SAY

"I'm not sure why, but I really like him/her."

ITS IMPACT ON OUR OPENNESS TO OTHERS

Opens us

OUR REACTION OR IMPULSE FOR ACTION IS...

To be attracted

RELATED EMOTIONS

Attraction, adoration, infatuation

ITS PURPOSE IS TO...

Draw us closer

THE TIME ORIENTATION OF THIS EMOTION IS...

Present

HOW THIS EMOTION CAN GET IN THE WAY

Enchantment literally means I feel as if I'm "under a spell." That will mean I'm not grounded with the reality of day-to-day needs and activities, which could sometimes be a barrier.

EMOTIONS WE CONFUSE IT WITH

Infatuation. Enchantment means to feel as if a spell has been cast over you. Infatuation is to act in a way that may make you look like a fool.

HOW IT FEELS OR MOVES US

To be under the spell of another

HOW OUR BODY MIGHT FEEL

Tingly, flushed, energized

HOW OUR BREATH MIGHT BE

Elevated pace, up in the chest

HOW OUR BODY MIGHT SHAPE ITSELF

Eyes wide open, chest open, leaning towards

QUOTE

"Whatever deceives men seems to produce a magical enchantment."—Plato

ENTHUSIASM

ETYMOLOGICAL ROOT

From Greek *enthousiasmos*, "divine inspiration," from *entheos* "divinely inspired, possessed by a god," from *en* "in" + *theos* "god"

WHAT WE THINK OR SAY

"I'm committed to a cause greater than myself."

ITS IMPACT ON OUR OPENNESS TO OTHERS

Opens us

OUR REACTION OR IMPULSE FOR ACTION IS...

To act on behalf of a cause, mission, or vision greater than yourself

RELATED EMOTIONS

Ambition, ebullience, passion, exuberance, boldness

ITS PURPOSE IS TO...

Allow us to connect with and be energized by a purpose or mission greater than ourselves

THE TIME ORIENTATION OF THIS EMOTION IS...

Future

HOW THIS EMOTION CAN GET IN THE WAY

Although it is an essential emotion for doing bold and challenging things, it can be difficult for others to connect or understand the mission as we do. This can create a gap in understanding and, at times, friction between leaders and their team.

EMOTIONS WE CONFUSE IT WITH

Ambition is to see possibilities and want to take advantage of them. Ambition tends to be more self-focused, while enthusiasm is focused on a vision or mission.

HOW IT FEELS OR MOVES US

To work toward fulfilling a mission

HOW OUR BODY MIGHT FEEL

Energized, ready to go

HOW OUR BREATH MIGHT BE

Fast and in the upper chest

HOW OUR BODY MIGHT SHAPE ITSELF

Tendency to move up and forward, eyes bright, face relaxed and open

QUOTE

"Enthusiasm is everything. It must be taut and vibrating like a guitar string."—Pele

ENTITLEMENT

ETYMOLOGICAL ROOT

From Late Latin *intitulare*, "give a title or name to," from *in-* "in" + *titulus* "title"

WHAT WE THINK OR SAY

"I believe the world owes me that."

ITS IMPACT ON OUR OPENNESS TO OTHERS

Closes us

OUR REACTION OR IMPULSE FOR ACTION IS…

Whine about what you do not have

RELATED EMOTIONS

Resentment, righteousness, arrogance

ITS PURPOSE IS TO…

Show me how life would be if I'd designed it

THE TIME ORIENTATION OF THIS EMOTION IS…

Present

HOW THIS EMOTION CAN GET IN THE WAY

Entitlement comes from the belief that "the world owes me the life I think I should have." If a mood, it will lead to dissatisfaction, disappointment, and often resentment.

EMOTIONS WE CONFUSE IT WITH

Greed. Greed is the emotion that has us take even when it is not needed. Entitlement means we believe "the world owes us" in some way.

HOW IT FEELS OR MOVES US

To whine

HOW OUR BODY MIGHT FEEL

Heavy

HOW OUR BREATH MIGHT BE

Slow and shallow

HOW OUR BODY MIGHT SHAPE ITSELF

Head lowered, shoulders stooped, chest concave

QUOTE

"I am afraid of privilege, of ease, of entitlement."—Tan Le

ENVY

The emotion is...........................

ETYMOLOGICAL ROOT

Latin from *invidere*, "to envy, hate," earlier "look at (with malice), cast an evil eye upon," from *in-* "upon" + *videre* "to see"

WHAT WE THINK OR SAY

"I would like to have what that person has."

ITS IMPACT ON OUR OPENNESS TO OTHERS

Closes us

OUR REACTION OR IMPULSE FOR ACTION IS...

Look for a way to include the thing I desire in my life

RELATED EMOTIONS

Admiration, covetousness, jealousy

ITS PURPOSE IS TO...

Show us what we would like to have as part of our life that we do not

THE TIME ORIENTATION OF THIS EMOTION IS...

Future

HOW THIS EMOTION CAN GET IN THE WAY

Envy is to look at our lives and see what is missing that others have. It is a comparative emotion which puts us into a form of competition with others. Due to that, it is not restful but is an emotion designed to disturb and challenge our status quo.

EMOTIONS WE CONFUSE IT WITH

Jealousy. Envy means we see something in another's life that we believe would enhance ours, while jealousy is the fear we will lose a relationship we care about. Envy is also confused with covetousness, which means wanting to take the thing we are attracted to.

HOW IT FEELS OR MOVES US

Desiring something we don't possess, often accompanied by an empty feeling

HOW OUR BODY MIGHT FEEL

Ungrounded

HOW OUR BREATH MIGHT BE

High in the chest, medium-paced

HOW OUR BODY MIGHT SHAPE ITSELF

Leaning towards what you are wanting, up and forward

QUOTE

"Do not overrate what you have received, nor envy others. He who envies others does not obtain peace of mind."
—Buddha

131

EQUANIMITY

The emotion is...

ETYMOLOGICAL ROOT

From Latin *aequanimitatem*, "evenness of mind, calmness; goodwill, kindness"

WHAT WE THINK OR SAY

"I feel balanced, centered, and able to look at all sides of the situation."

ITS IMPACT ON OUR OPENNESS TO OTHERS

Neutral

OUR REACTION OR IMPULSE FOR ACTION IS...

To consider in a calm and evenhanded manner

RELATED EMOTIONS

Dispassion, peace, calmness, acceptance

ITS PURPOSE IS TO...

Allow us to consider things from a balanced emotional state

THE TIME ORIENTATION OF THIS EMOTION IS...

Present

HOW THIS EMOTION CAN GET IN THE WAY

Equanimity can be identified by the calmness it generates. It is a peaceful and restful emotion, but does not produce action and cannot react to danger or threats.

EMOTIONS WE CONFUSE IT WITH

Peace. Equanimity means we feel all things are balanced, whereas peace is the absence of conflict.

HOW IT FEELS OR MOVES US

To remain balanced and centered

HOW OUR BODY MIGHT FEEL

Completely relaxed and yet alert

HOW OUR BREATH MIGHT BE

Even, steady, belly breathing

HOW OUR BODY MIGHT SHAPE ITSELF

Open and full length, width, and depth

QUOTE

"Victory and defeat are a part of life, which are to be viewed with equanimity."—Atal Bihari Vajpayee

EROTICISM

ETYMOLOGICAL ROOT

From Greek *erotikos*, "caused by passionate love, referring to love," from *eros* "sexual love"

WHAT WE THINK OR SAY

"I desire to become one with another."

ITS IMPACT ON OUR OPENNESS TO OTHERS

Opens us

OUR REACTION OR IMPULSE FOR ACTION IS...

To meld with another

RELATED EMOTIONS

Lust, passion, desire

ITS PURPOSE IS TO...

Let us unite as one

THE TIME ORIENTATION OF THIS EMOTION IS...

Present

HOW THIS EMOTION CAN GET IN THE WAY

Eroticism is an intense desire to "become one" with another, particularly sexually. The attraction of that can lead us into relationships outside our personal or social commitments and values.

EMOTIONS WE CONFUSE IT WITH

Passion. Eroticism refers to joining in sexual relations, while passion is the desire to meld with another. Passion pertains to many areas outside of sex.

HOW IT FEELS OR MOVES US

We are powerfully drawn physically and sexually to another.

HOW OUR BODY MIGHT FEEL

Warm, energized, energy streaming throughout the body

HOW OUR BREATH MIGHT BE

Fast, shallow

HOW OUR BODY MIGHT SHAPE ITSELF

Open, full length, width, and depth

QUOTE

"Eroticism is like a dance: one always leads the other."
—*Milan Kundera*

EUPHORIA

ETYMOLOGICAL ROOT

Greek *euphoria*, "power of enduring easily," from *euphoros*, literally "bearing well"

WHAT WE THINK OR SAY

"I feel extraordinary well-being."

OUR REACTION OR IMPULSE FOR ACTION IS...

To remain immersed in the experience as long as possible

ITS PURPOSE IS TO...

Connect us with what is highly pleasurable

ITS IMPACT ON OUR OPENNESS TO OTHERS

Opens us

RELATED EMOTIONS

Elation, ecstasy, exuberance, excitement

THE TIME ORIENTATION OF THIS EMOTION IS...

Present

HOW THIS EMOTION CAN GET IN THE WAY

Euphoria is an emotion that feels very good to us, and that can sometimes be a trap. The desire to remain in euphoria may lead us to actions out of alignment with our values.

EMOTIONS WE CONFUSE IT WITH

Excitement. Euphoria means "we feel no pain" and can sustain our activity. Excitement is the desire to experience higher and higher levels of energy.

HOW IT FEELS OR MOVES US

To throw ourselves into an experience

HOW OUR BODY MIGHT FEEL

Warm, gentle flowing energy

HOW OUR BREATH MIGHT BE

Medium pace, middle chest to belly breathing

HOW OUR BODY MIGHT SHAPE ITSELF

Open, smiling, full length, width, and depth

QUOTE

"Weightlessness was unbelievable. It's physical euphoria: Nothing about you has any weight. You don't realize that you are weighed down all the time by yourself, and your organs, and your head."—Mary Roach

EXCITEMENT

ETYMOLOGICAL ROOT

From Latin *excitare*, "rouse, call out, summon forth, produce"

WHAT WE THINK OR SAY

"I love this."

ITS IMPACT ON OUR OPENNESS TO OTHERS

Opens us

OUR REACTION OR IMPULSE FOR ACTION IS...

To do more or again

RELATED EMOTIONS

Enthusiasm, anticipation, delight, elation

ITS PURPOSE IS TO...

Elevate our energy level

THE TIME ORIENTATION OF THIS EMOTION IS...

Present

HOW THIS EMOTION CAN GET IN THE WAY

Excitement is a high level of energy somatically that feels, at times, close to euphoria. Excitement, by its nature, requires increasing levels of stimulation to maintain, which can make it addictive.

EMOTIONS WE CONFUSE IT WITH

Enthusiasm. Excitement is the emotion in which our energy spills out of us, whereas enthusiasm is the emotion in which we are connected with a greater purpose or divine mission.

HOW IT FEELS OR MOVES US

We have high energy and look for ways to maintain it.

HOW OUR BODY MIGHT FEEL

Flushed, warm to hot temperature, very energized

HOW OUR BREATH MIGHT BE

Fast-paced, high in the upper chest

HOW OUR BODY MIGHT SHAPE ITSELF

Tendency to move up and forward, open, full length, depth, and width

QUOTE

"Excitement was plentiful during my two years' service as a Pony Express rider."—Buffalo Bill

EXHILARATION

The emotion

ETYMOLOGICAL ROOT

Latin *ex-* "thoroughly" + *hilarare* "make cheerful"

WHAT WE THINK OR SAY

"I'm extremely happy."

ITS IMPACT ON OUR OPENNESS TO OTHERS

Opens us

OUR REACTION OR IMPULSE FOR ACTION IS...

To enjoy with heightened awareness

RELATED EMOTIONS

Euphoria, ecstasy, exuberance, excitement

ITS PURPOSE IS TO...

Allow us to celebrate and appreciate life's experiences

THE TIME ORIENTATION OF THIS EMOTION IS...

Present

HOW THIS EMOTION CAN GET IN THE WAY

To be exhilarated is to experience "enormous happiness." Although that is a deeply enjoyable experience, it can cause us to overlook the pain and suffering of others—or even, at times, our own.

EMOTIONS WE CONFUSE IT WITH

Excitement. Exhilarated means we are thoroughly cheerful. Excitement is feeling elevated energy for a situation or project.

HOW IT FEELS OR MOVES US

We are breathless with joy.

HOW OUR BODY MIGHT FEEL

Energized and flush

HOW OUR BREATH MIGHT BE

High in the chest, fast-paced

HOW OUR BODY MIGHT SHAPE ITSELF

Moving up and forward, full length and width

QUOTE

"All of us are living with dogmas that we accept as truths. When one of these is overturned, there's an initial gasp, soon followed by a rush of exhilaration."—Deepak Chopra

EXPECTANCY

ETYMOLOGICAL ROOT

From Latin *expectare*, "await, look out for; desire, hope, long for"

WHAT WE THINK OR SAY

"I'm waiting for something to happen."

ITS IMPACT ON OUR OPENNESS TO OTHERS

Opens us

OUR REACTION OR IMPULSE FOR ACTION IS...

Focus on unfolding events

RELATED EMOTIONS

Anticipation, anxiety, desire

ITS PURPOSE IS TO...

Show us what we believe is about to happen

THE TIME ORIENTATION OF THIS EMOTION IS...

Future

HOW THIS EMOTION CAN GET IN THE WAY

Expectancy, by nature, is focused on the future. This alone means we will miss what is occurring in the present.

EMOTIONS WE CONFUSE IT WITH

Anxiety. Expectant means we are waiting for something good or desirable to happen. Anxiety is waiting for something to happen that we believe may harm us.

HOW IT FEELS OR MOVES US

We wait.

HOW OUR BODY MIGHT FEEL

Agitated, energized, restless, wanting to move

HOW OUR BREATH MIGHT BE

Short, high in the chest, shallow

HOW OUR BODY MIGHT SHAPE ITSELF

Moving towards, open, expanded length

"Expectant waiting is the foundation of the spiritual life."—*Simone Weil*

143

EXUBERANCE

ETYMOLOGICAL ROOT

From Latin *exuberantem*, "overabundance"

WHAT WE THINK OR SAY

"Life is abundant."

ITS IMPACT ON OUR OPENNESS TO OTHERS

Opens us

OUR REACTION OR IMPULSE FOR ACTION IS...

To throw yourself into life

RELATED EMOTIONS

Euphoria, exhilaration, ecstasy

ITS PURPOSE IS TO...

Understand how abundant life can be

THE TIME ORIENTATION OF THIS EMOTION IS...

Present

HOW THIS EMOTION CAN GET IN THE WAY

Exuberance means to live in overabundance, which can mean that we are receiving so many gifts we are unable to keep track of them all. In other words, we are overwhelmed with the generosity of the universe.

EMOTIONS WE CONFUSE IT WITH

Enthusiasm. Exuberance means we are experiencing an overabundance of something or we are overwhelmed in a good way. Enthusiasm means we are connected with a mission or divine purpose.

HOW IT FEELS OR MOVES US

We have an almost over-whelming urge to participate and experience life.

HOW OUR BODY MIGHT FEEL

Very energized

HOW OUR BREATH MIGHT BE

Fast, high in the chest

HOW OUR BODY MIGHT SHAPE ITSELF

A desire to jump up and down, open, expanded in all three dimensions: length, width, and depth

QUOTE

"The body energy that we feel in fear is the same body energy we feel when excited, the only difference is the anticipated outcome of the situation" —*Curtis Watkins*

FAITH

The emotion is......................

ETYMOLOGICAL ROOT

From Latin *fides*, "trust, reliance, credence, belief"

WHAT WE THINK OR SAY

"I believe it even though I don't have any evidence it is true."

ITS IMPACT ON OUR OPENNESS TO OTHERS

Opens us

OUR REACTION OR IMPULSE FOR ACTION IS...

To commit to a belief

RELATED EMOTIONS

Trust, reverence, hope

ITS PURPOSE IS TO...

Allow us to believe without relying on evidence

THE TIME ORIENTATION OF THIS EMOTION IS...

Present or future

HOW THIS EMOTION CAN GET IN THE WAY

Faith allows us to believe "whatever we want," which is useful but can lead us astray as well.

EMOTIONS WE CONFUSE IT WITH

Hope. Faith means we believe something even though we cannot show evidence it is true. Hope is the desire that something good will happen.

HOW IT FEELS OR MOVES US

To steadfastly believe

HOW OUR BODY MIGHT FEEL

Peaceful, calm, relaxed

HOW OUR BREATH MIGHT BE

Deep and even

HOW OUR BODY MIGHT SHAPE ITSELF

Chest open, head up, length, width, and depth full

QUOTE

"Faith is to believe what you do not see; the reward of this faith is to see what you believe."—Saint Augustine

FASCINATION

ETYMOLOGICAL ROOT

Fascinationem, from Latin, meaning "bewitch, enchant"

WHAT WE THINK OR SAY

"I can't take my eyes off him/her/it."

ITS IMPACT ON OUR OPENNESS TO OTHERS

Opens us

OUR REACTION OR IMPULSE FOR ACTION IS...

To pay singular attention to something or someone

RELATED EMOTIONS

Wonder, incredulity, curiosity

ITS PURPOSE IS TO...

Focus our attention on what is interesting

THE TIME ORIENTATION OF THIS EMOTION IS...

Present

HOW THIS EMOTION CAN GET IN THE WAY

Fascination is an intense interest, to the degree that we cannot look away. Since it takes all our attention, we can be sure we miss other things that could be equally important.

EMOTIONS WE CONFUSE IT WITH

Intrigued. In fascination we feel bewitched or enchanted; when we feel intrigued, we feel entangled in something because we are so interested in it.

HOW IT FEELS OR MOVES US

Our attention is riveted.

HOW OUR BODY MIGHT FEEL

Energized

HOW OUR BREATH MIGHT BE

Fast-paced, mid-chest area

HOW OUR BODY MIGHT SHAPE ITSELF

Wide-eyed, open

QUOTE

"I have trouble with modern art. But in general, all art forms fascinate me—art is the way human beings express what we can't say in words."—Andrea Bocelli

FEAR

The emotion is.........................

ETYMOLOGICAL ROOT

From Old English *fær*, "calamity, sudden danger, peril, sudden attack"

WHAT WE THINK OR SAY

"I believe something may harm me, and I'm clear what it is."

ITS IMPACT ON OUR OPENNESS TO OTHERS

Closes us

OUR REACTION OR IMPULSE FOR ACTION IS...

To avoid perceived danger

RELATED EMOTIONS

Anxiety, doubt, dread

ITS PURPOSE IS TO...

Help us avoid danger

THE TIME ORIENTATION OF THIS EMOTION IS...

Future

HOW THIS EMOTION CAN GET IN THE WAY

Fear, when it becomes a mood, causes us to be hypervigilant and always looking for possible danger. From that energy, it is impossible to take risks or stray from a narrow path we consider safe enough.

EMOTIONS WE CONFUSE IT WITH

Anxiety. Fear is the belief that we may be harmed by something or someone specific, as in "getting hit by a bus," whereas anxiety is the belief we may be harmed, but the source is vague or unidentified.

HOW IT FEELS OR MOVES US

We run away or freeze in order to avoid danger.

HOW OUR BODY MIGHT FEEL

Tightness in belly, chest, and jaw

HOW OUR BREATH MIGHT BE

Shallow and fast

HOW OUR BODY MIGHT SHAPE ITSELF

Hunched over, chest concave, tendency to move away

QUOTE

"I learned that courage was not the absence of fear, but the triumph over it. The brave man is not he who does not feel afraid, but he who conquers that fear."—Nelson Mandela

FRUSTRATION

ETYMOLOGICAL ROOT

From Latin *frustrationem*, "a deception, a disappointment"

WHAT WE THINK OR SAY

"It should've already happened; it shouldn't be this hard."

ITS IMPACT ON OUR OPENNESS TO OTHERS

Closes us

OUR REACTION OR IMPULSE FOR ACTION IS...

To look for a faster or simpler way

RELATED EMOTIONS

Irritation, anger, annoyance

ITS PURPOSE IS TO...

Challenge us to find a simpler or faster way

THE TIME ORIENTATION OF THIS EMOTION IS...

Present

HOW THIS EMOTION CAN GET IN THE WAY

Frustration means we believe there must be a faster or easier way to do something. Often we believe it means something is wrong, which can cause us to look for someone to blame even when it is not warranted.

EMOTIONS WE CONFUSE IT WITH

Anger. Frustration means "I think this is taking too long or is too difficult," whereas anger comes from encountering what we believe to be unjust.

HOW IT FEELS OR MOVES US

We look for alternatives.

HOW OUR BODY MIGHT FEEL

Tightness in the jaw and shoulders

HOW OUR BREATH MIGHT BE

Fast, shallow

HOW OUR BODY MIGHT SHAPE ITSELF

Tendency to move against, diminished length

QUOTE

"Expectation is the mother of all frustration."
—Antonio Banderas

153

FURY

The emotion is......................

ETYMOLOGICAL ROOT

From Latin *furia*, "violent passion, rage, madness"

WHAT WE THINK OR SAY

"Nothing will stop me attacking."

ITS IMPACT ON OUR OPENNESS TO OTHERS

Closes us

OUR REACTION OR IMPULSE FOR ACTION IS...

To attack with all your energy

RELATED EMOTIONS

Rage, anger, lust

ITS PURPOSE IS TO...

Let us attack

THE TIME ORIENTATION OF THIS EMOTION IS...

Present

HOW THIS EMOTION CAN GET IN THE WAY

Fury is violent madness and has no limits, so it can be very destructive.

EMOTIONS WE CONFUSE IT WITH

Rage. Fury is a "violent madness," whereas rage is the belief that nothing is worth saving and therefore should be destroyed.

HOW IT FEELS OR MOVES US

We feel like attacking the source.

HOW OUR BODY MIGHT FEEL

Hot, flashes of energy

HOW OUR BREATH MIGHT BE

High in the chest, very rapid pace

HOW OUR BODY MIGHT SHAPE ITSELF

Fists clenched, jaw clenched, tendency to move against

QUOTE

"I had had a continuing smoldering fury about the treatment of Jews in Germany."—*J. Robert Oppenheimer*

GENEROSITY

ETYMOLOGICAL ROOT

From Latin *generosus*, "of noble birth," figuratively "magnanimous, generous"

WHAT WE THINK OR SAY

"I want to share what I have."

ITS IMPACT ON OUR OPENNESS TO OTHERS

Opens us

OUR REACTION OR IMPULSE FOR ACTION IS...

To give

RELATED EMOTIONS

Magnanimity, kindness, gratitude

ITS PURPOSE IS TO...

Allow us to share our wealth or resources

THE TIME ORIENTATION OF THIS EMOTION IS...

Past, present, or future

HOW THIS EMOTION CAN GET IN THE WAY

If we give overgenerously of our money or time, we may find we are left without sufficient resources to take care of ourselves.

EMOTIONS WE CONFUSE IT WITH

Kindness. Generosity is the emotion that allows us to share our resources with others, whereas kindness is treating people well. Both occur without the expectation of them being acknowledged or returned.

HOW IT FEELS OR MOVES US

We feel like giving to others.

HOW OUR BODY MIGHT FEEL

Warm, gentle flowing energy

HOW OUR BREATH MIGHT BE

Long, slow, deep breaths

HOW OUR BODY MIGHT SHAPE ITSELF

Open, arms reaching out, smile

QUOTE

"Gentleness, self-sacrifice and generosity are the exclusive possession of no one race or religion."—Mahatma Gandhi

157

GRATITUDE

ETYMOLOGICAL ROOT

From Latin *gratia*, "favor, esteem, regard; pleasing quality, goodwill"

WHAT WE THINK OR SAY

"Life and everything that is a part of it is a gift."

ITS IMPACT ON OUR OPENNESS TO OTHERS

Opens us

OUR REACTION OR IMPULSE FOR ACTION IS...

To appreciate all that I've received for free

RELATED EMOTIONS

Thankfulness, appreciation

ITS PURPOSE IS TO...

Make us realize that even life is a gift and not something we have earned or even deserve

THE TIME ORIENTATION OF THIS EMOTION IS...

Present

HOW THIS EMOTION CAN GET IN THE WAY

Since gratitude is the belief everything is a gift, it can blind us to evil intentions or destructive actions of others.

EMOTIONS WE CONFUSE IT WITH

Thankfulness. Gratitude is to believe everything is a gift and we did not receive it in exchange for anything. Thankfulness is appreciation of an equal exchange.

HOW IT FEELS OR MOVES US

To give thanks, appreciate, and reflect on our good fortune

HOW OUR BODY MIGHT FEEL

Tingling, warm, uplifted

HOW OUR BREATH MIGHT BE

Steady, deep

HOW OUR BODY MIGHT SHAPE ITSELF

Open, chest full in the front and back, connected to above and below, front and back, left and right

QUOTE

"I don't have to chase extraordinary moments to find happiness—it's right in front of me if I'm paying attention and practicing gratitude."—Brené Brown

GREED

ETYMOLOGICAL ROOT

Old English *grædig* (West Saxon), *gredig* (Anglian),
"voracious, hungry," also "covetous, eager to obtain"

WHAT WE THINK OR SAY

"I may not need it, but I'm
going to take it anyway."

ITS IMPACT ON OUR OPENNESS TO OTHERS

Closes us

OUR REACTION OR IMPULSE FOR ACTION IS...

To take

RELATED EMOTIONS

Fear

ITS PURPOSE IS TO...

Let us collect and gather regardless
of need

THE TIME ORIENTATION OF THIS EMOTION IS...

Present

HOW THIS EMOTION CAN GET IN THE WAY

Greed means to take all we can regardless of need and has obvious consequences in terms of sharing resources. It may also result in us having so much we have no way to store or manage it.

EMOTIONS WE CONFUSE IT WITH

Covetousness. Greed is the emotion that provokes us to take regardless of whether we need it. Covetousness is the desire to take away something specific that someone else has.

HOW IT FEELS OR MOVES US

We want to take or gather as much as we can.

HOW OUR BODY MIGHT FEEL

Tight in the belly and heart

HOW OUR BREATH MIGHT BE

High in the chest and shallow

HOW OUR BODY MIGHT SHAPE ITSELF

Width and depth are diminished

QUOTE

"It is greed to do all the talking but not to want to listen at all."—Democritus

GUILT

The emotion is.........................

ETYMOLOGICAL ROOT

Old English *gylt*, "crime, sin, fault, fine," of unknown origin

WHAT WE THINK OR SAY

"In doing that, I broke my own standards."

ITS IMPACT ON OUR OPENNESS TO OTHERS

Closes us

OUR REACTION OR IMPULSE FOR ACTION IS...

To blame and punish myself

RELATED EMOTIONS

Shame, embarrassment, shyness

ITS PURPOSE IS TO...

Take care of our private identity

THE TIME ORIENTATION OF THIS EMOTION IS...

Past

HOW THIS EMOTION CAN GET IN THE WAY

Guilt, if understood as a guide to keep us acting out of our personal values, is a helpful emotion. When we cannot exit guilt, we may continue to punish ourselves for things long past.

EMOTIONS WE CONFUSE IT WITH

Shame. Guilt is the realization that we have betrayed our personal values or haven't acted consistent with our beliefs. Shame means the same in regard to group or community values and beliefs.

HOW IT FEELS OR MOVES US

We feel like punishing ourself for breaking a personal value.

HOW OUR BODY MIGHT FEEL

Heavy

HOW OUR BREATH MIGHT BE

Slow and shallow

HOW OUR BODY MIGHT SHAPE ITSELF

Collapsed into itself, head down, shoulders slumped, concave chest

QUOTE

"Nothing is more wretched than the mind of a man conscious of guilt."—Plautus

HAPPINESS

ETYMOLOGICAL ROOT

Old English, late 14c., "lucky, favored by fortune, prosperous;" of events, "turning out well"

WHAT WE THINK OR SAY

"Life is good."

ITS IMPACT ON OUR OPENNESS TO OTHERS

Opens us

OUR REACTION OR IMPULSE FOR ACTION IS...

To enjoy the moment

RELATED EMOTIONS

Delight, joy, bliss, euphoria

ITS PURPOSE IS TO...

Show us what a good life looks like

THE TIME ORIENTATION OF THIS EMOTION IS...

Present

HOW THIS EMOTION CAN GET IN THE WAY

Happiness is related to joy and contentment and is a pleasant emotion to feel; however, we will only appreciate it when we also have the experience of sadness or disappointment.

EMOTIONS WE CONFUSE IT WITH

Joy. Happiness is the belief that things are "turning out well" or happening in a way that pleases us. Joy is the emotion that allows us to celebrate all that is good in life.

HOW IT FEELS OR MOVES US

We feel content and would like things to continue as they are.

HOW OUR BODY MIGHT FEEL

Light, energized, flowing

HOW OUR BREATH MIGHT BE

Moderate pace, mid-chest

HOW OUR BODY MIGHT SHAPE ITSELF

Open, head tilted perhaps, smile, chest relaxed and open

QUOTE

"Be happy for this moment. This moment is your life."
—*Omar Khayyam*

165

HATE

ETYMOLOGICAL ROOT

Old English hatian, "regard with extreme ill-will, have a passionate aversion to, treat as an enemy"

WHAT WE THINK OR SAY

"I cannot stand being around that person."

ITS IMPACT ON OUR OPENNESS TO OTHERS

Closes us

OUR REACTION OR IMPULSE FOR ACTION IS...

To avoid

RELATED EMOTIONS

Disgust, contempt, revulsion

ITS PURPOSE IS TO...

Distinguish who we don't want to be near or what we don't want to be part of

THE TIME ORIENTATION OF THIS EMOTION IS...

Present

166

HOW THIS EMOTION CAN GET IN THE WAY

Since hate makes us want to be as far from something or someone as possible, it keeps us from knowing about them, and possibly, preparing ourselves should we need to interact with them.

EMOTIONS WE CONFUSE IT WITH

Anger. Many people have an interpretation that hate means wanting to hurt or punish, but the predisposition of hate is to stay as far away as possible. It is the predisposition of anger that is to punish the source of injustice.

HOW IT FEELS OR MOVES US

We feel like avoiding or staying away from who or what we hate.

HOW OUR BODY MIGHT FEEL

Tight in the neck, shoulders, and belly

HOW OUR BREATH MIGHT BE

High in the chest, slow to medium pace

HOW OUR BODY MIGHT SHAPE ITSELF

Face contorted, scrunched together, eyes narrowed and focused, shoulders hunched, chest concave

QUOTE

"From the deepest desires often come the deadliest hate."
—Socrates

HILARITY

ETYMOLOGICAL ROOT

From Latin *hilaritatem*, "cheerfulness, gaiety, merriment"

WHAT WE THINK OR SAY

"This is tremendously funny."

ITS IMPACT ON OUR OPENNESS TO OTHERS

Opens us

OUR REACTION OR IMPULSE FOR ACTION IS...

To laugh

RELATED EMOTIONS

Delight, joy, happiness

ITS PURPOSE IS TO...

Allow unfettered enjoyment

THE TIME ORIENTATION OF THIS EMOTION IS...

Present

HOW THIS EMOTION CAN GET IN THE WAY

Hilarity in circumstances of amusement and play is perfectly suited. However, there are many contexts in which hilarity would be considered disrespectful, such as funerals, worship services, and serious meetings.

EMOTIONS WE CONFUSE IT WITH

Irreverence. Hilarity is the emotion in which everything in life is funny and we are merry. Irreverence is the emotion that keeps us from taking things overly seriously or with gravitas.

HOW IT FEELS OR MOVES US

We can't stop laughing.

HOW OUR BODY MIGHT FEEL

Energized, light

HOW OUR BREATH MIGHT BE

Fast, belly breathing

HOW OUR BODY MIGHT SHAPE ITSELF

Open

 **QUOTE**

"Fan the sinking flame of hilarity with the wing of friendship: And pass the rosy wine."—Charles Dickens

HONOR

ETYMOLOGICAL ROOT

From Latin *honorem*, "dignity, office, reputation"

WHAT WE THINK OR SAY

"I feel my status has been acknowledged."

ITS IMPACT ON OUR OPENNESS TO OTHERS

Opens us

OUR REACTION OR IMPULSE FOR ACTION IS...

To act according to tradition

RELATED EMOTIONS

Respect, dignity

ITS PURPOSE IS TO...

Respect and follow traditional ways

THE TIME ORIENTATION OF THIS EMOTION IS...

Present

HOW THIS EMOTION CAN GET IN THE WAY

Honor requires that things be done in a certain formal way. There may be times when this is not possible, but the need for that can keep us stuck.

EMOTIONS WE CONFUSE IT WITH

Dignity. Both have to do with our personal identity, but honor is doing things as we believe they should be done and dignity is believing that we have the legitimate right to make that decision.

HOW IT FEELS OR MOVES US

We acknowledge tradition through rituals.

HOW OUR BODY MIGHT FEEL

Relaxed and open

HOW OUR BREATH MIGHT BE

Long, slow, and deep

HOW OUR BODY MIGHT SHAPE ITSELF

Head slightly lowered; otherwise length is full

QUOTE

"I would prefer even to fail with honor than win by cheating."—*Sophocles*

HOPE

ETYMOLOGICAL ROOT

Old English *hopian*, "wish, expect, look forward (to something)," of unknown origin

WHAT WE THINK OR SAY

"I believe the future will be better than the present or the past."

ITS IMPACT ON OUR OPENNESS TO OTHERS

Opens us

OUR REACTION OR IMPULSE FOR ACTION IS...

To look to the future

RELATED EMOTIONS

Optimism, enthusiasm, ambition

ITS PURPOSE IS TO...

Allow us to envision a better future

THE TIME ORIENTATION OF THIS EMOTION IS...

Future

HOW THIS EMOTION CAN GET IN THE WAY

Hope can get in the way when it is naïve or denies reality. It is not unusual to ignore facts when hope takes over.

EMOTIONS WE CONFUSE IT WITH

Naïveté. Hope is the belief that the future will be better in some way than the past, whereas naïveté is the belief that life should be the way I want it to be.

HOW IT FEELS OR MOVES US

We think about the future and how it could be good.

HOW OUR BODY MIGHT FEEL

Elevated

HOW OUR BREATH MIGHT BE

Even, slow, deep

HOW OUR BODY MIGHT SHAPE ITSELF

Length is extended

QUOTE

"We must accept finite disappointment, but never lose infinite hope."—Martin Luther King Jr.

HOPELESSNESS

ETYMOLOGICAL ROOT

Old English *hopian*, "wish, expect, look forward (to something)" + *leas* "lacking, cannot be, does not"

WHAT WE THINK OR SAY

"I cannot imagine a future better than the present."

ITS IMPACT ON OUR OPENNESS TO OTHERS

Closes us

OUR REACTION OR IMPULSE FOR ACTION IS…

Withdraw and do nothing

RELATED EMOTIONS

Despair, resignation

ITS PURPOSE IS TO…

Allow us to let go of trying to create a better future

THE TIME ORIENTATION OF THIS EMOTION IS…

Future

HOW THIS EMOTION CAN GET IN THE WAY

Hopelessness is the belief that there can be no good future and possibly no future at all. Given that, we have no impetus to attempt any actions of any kind. We are immobilized.

EMOTIONS WE CONFUSE IT WITH

Resignation. Hopelessness is the belief that the future will not be an improvement on the past, whereas resignation is the belief that nothing I do will make any difference. Both lead to inaction, but for different reasons.

HOW IT FEELS OR MOVES US

Heavy in the chest

HOW OUR BODY MIGHT FEEL

Heavy, lethargic

HOW OUR BREATH MIGHT BE

Short, shallow, deep sighs

HOW OUR BODY MIGHT SHAPE ITSELF

Shoulders slumped, head down, gaze is down

QUOTE

"Nothing prompts creativity like poverty, a feeling of hopelessness, and a bit of panic."—Catherine Tate

HORROR

ETYMOLOGICAL ROOT

From Latin *horror*, literally "a shaking, trembling, shudder, chill," from *horrere*, "to bristle with fear, shudder"

WHAT WE THINK OR SAY

"I can't imagine anything worse."

ITS IMPACT ON OUR OPENNESS TO OTHERS

Closes us

OUR REACTION OR IMPULSE FOR ACTION IS...

To tremble and freeze

RELATED EMOTIONS

Terror, dread, fear

ITS PURPOSE IS TO...

Know the worst of what is possible

THE TIME ORIENTATION OF THIS EMOTION IS...

Past, present, or future

HOW THIS EMOTION CAN GET IN THE WAY

Horror drives us or keeps us away from a scene. If our work or duty is to be at that place, it can restrict us from fulfilling our obligations.

EMOTIONS WE CONFUSE IT WITH

Terror. Horror is a fear of our worst fears, whereas terror is the expectation of something terrible happening.

HOW IT FEELS OR MOVES US

Makes us want to run and hide, or at least close our eyes

HOW OUR BODY MIGHT FEEL

Tight in the belly and face

HOW OUR BREATH MIGHT BE

Stopped, fitful, deep sudden inhales

HOW OUR BODY MIGHT SHAPE ITSELF

Face is scrunched, length and width are diminished significantly

QUOTE

"Where there is no imagination there is no horror."
—*Arthur Conan Doyle*

HUBRIS

ETYMOLOGICAL ROOT

From Greek *hybris*, "wanton violence, insolence, outrage," originally "presumption toward the gods"

WHAT WE THINK OR SAY

"I'm untouchable and therefore can act however I choose."

ITS IMPACT ON OUR OPENNESS TO OTHERS

Closes us

OUR REACTION OR IMPULSE FOR ACTION IS...

To act believing there will not be consequences

RELATED EMOTIONS

Arrogance, pride

ITS PURPOSE IS TO...

Act without consideration of consequences

THE TIME ORIENTATION OF THIS EMOTION IS...

Present

HOW THIS EMOTION CAN GET IN THE WAY

Hubris is the belief we are untouchable and godlike. This can obviously get in the way when we are dealing with other mortals who do not see us as divine or near-divine.

EMOTIONS WE CONFUSE IT WITH

Arrogance. The root of hubris means to imagine ourselves as among the gods or beyond being human, while arrogance is that we are human but superior to the rest of humanity.

HOW IT FEELS OR MOVES US

We act without regard to consequences.

HOW OUR BODY MIGHT FEEL

Energized, powerful

HOW OUR BREATH MIGHT BE

Full, chest breathing

HOW OUR BODY MIGHT SHAPE ITSELF

Full length, width, and depth

QUOTE

"Hubris is one of the great renewable resources."
—*P. J. O'Rourke*

HUMILITY

ETYMOLOGICAL ROOT

From Latin *humilis*, "lowly, humble," literally "on the ground," from *humus*, "earth"

WHAT WE THINK OR SAY

"I claim exactly who and what I am—nothing more, nothing less."

ITS IMPACT ON OUR OPENNESS TO OTHERS

Opens us

OUR REACTION OR IMPULSE FOR ACTION IS...

To recognize our limits

RELATED EMOTIONS

Obsequiousness

ITS PURPOSE IS TO...

Ground us in reality

THE TIME ORIENTATION OF THIS EMOTION IS...

Present

HOW THIS EMOTION CAN GET IN THE WAY

In humility it is impossible to brag or make ourselves out to be more than we are. It is even difficult to do playfully, so we cannot experiment with being more.

EMOTIONS WE CONFUSE IT WITH

Obsequiousness. Humility is the emotion that keeps us grounded in terms of our beliefs about ourselves, whereas in obsequiousness we believe we are less important than others.

HOW IT FEELS OR MOVES US

We are quiet and reserved, never bragging or calling attention to ourselves.

HOW OUR BODY MIGHT FEEL

Relaxed, warm, open

HOW OUR BREATH MIGHT BE

Even, slow, medium-depth breathing

HOW OUR BODY MIGHT SHAPE ITSELF

Open chest, head slightly bent down, eyes open and clear

QUOTE

"Humility is the solid foundation of all virtues."
—Confucius

IMPATIENCE

ETYMOLOGICAL ROOT

Latin *in-* "not," + *patientia*, "endurance, submission"

WHAT WE THINK OR SAY

"I am ready, but others are not."

ITS IMPACT ON OUR OPENNESS TO OTHERS

Closes us

OUR REACTION OR IMPULSE FOR ACTION IS...

To look for a way around whatever is blocking us

RELATED EMOTIONS

Frustration, anger, ire

ITS PURPOSE IS TO...

Get into action

THE TIME ORIENTATION OF THIS EMOTION IS...

Present

HOW THIS EMOTION CAN GET IN THE WAY

Since impatience is based on a gap between our readiness and the readiness of others, it can get in the way when we blame this on others.

EMOTIONS WE CONFUSE IT WITH

Frustration. Impatience means "I am ready but others aren't," whereas frustration is the belief that things could move more rapidly. Related, definitely, but telling us something different.

HOW IT FEELS OR MOVES US

We are restless and ready to go.

HOW OUR BODY MIGHT FEEL

Agitated, tense, constricted

HOW OUR BREATH MIGHT BE

Shallow, fast-paced

HOW OUR BODY MIGHT SHAPE ITSELF

Forward leaning, length somewhat collapsed

QUOTE

"Youthful impatience obscures the endless potential for joy that's standing right in front of you."—Greg Gutfeld

INCREDULITY

ETYMOLOGICAL ROOT

From Latin *incredulus*, "unbelieving" from *in-* "not" + *credulous*, "worthy to be believed"

WHAT WE THINK OR SAY

"I can't believe it!"

ITS IMPACT ON OUR OPENNESS TO OTHERS

Closes us

OUR REACTION OR IMPULSE FOR ACTION IS…

To question how something could be possible

RELATED EMOTIONS

Disbelief, skepticism, doubt

ITS PURPOSE IS TO…

Acknowledge what is beyond belief

THE TIME ORIENTATION OF THIS EMOTION IS…

Present

HOW THIS EMOTION CAN GET IN THE WAY

Someone who is constantly incredulous probably lives with naïveté and does not see the world as it is but as they would like it to be. This can easily lead to disappointment.

EMOTIONS WE CONFUSE IT WITH

Skepticism. Incredulity is the state of being unable to believe something is true because it is so far removed from our experience; skepticism is the challenge of deciding which of two alternatives to believe—my current belief or something new I'm encountering.

HOW IT FEELS OR MOVES US

We struggle to make sense of the situation.

HOW OUR BODY MIGHT FEEL

Shaky

HOW OUR BREATH MIGHT BE

Fast, mid-chest

HOW OUR BODY MIGHT SHAPE ITSELF

Moving back and away, width diminished

QUOTE

"It is always well to accept your own shortcomings with candor but to regard those of your friends with polite incredulity."—Russell Lynes

INDIFFERENCE

ETYMOLOGICAL ROOT

From Latin *indifferentem*, "not differing, not particular, of no consequence, neither good nor evil"

WHAT WE THINK OR SAY

"It is all the same to me if we do x or if we do y."

ITS IMPACT ON OUR OPENNESS TO OTHERS

Neutral to closes us

OUR REACTION OR IMPULSE FOR ACTION IS...

To follow whatever others suggest

RELATED EMOTIONS

Boredom, ambivalence, apathy

ITS PURPOSE IS TO...

Give control of decision-making to others

THE TIME ORIENTATION OF THIS EMOTION IS...

Present

HOW THIS EMOTION CAN GET IN THE WAY

When indifferent, we don't recognize differences, with the result that good and evil and levels of quality and efficiency do not matter. This can have a profoundly negative effect on our lives and relationships.

EMOTIONS WE CONFUSE IT WITH

Boredom. Boredom is the inability to find any benefit in an activity, while indifference is not caring about an activity.

HOW IT FEELS OR MOVES US Lethargic and uncaring	**HOW OUR BODY MIGHT FEEL** Listless
HOW OUR BREATH MIGHT BE Shallow and light	**HOW OUR BODY MIGHT SHAPE ITSELF** Leaning back and down, width narrowed

QUOTE

"The opposite of love is not hate, it's indifference."
—*Elie Wiesel*

INDIGNATION

ETYMOLOGICAL ROOT

Latin from *indignus*, "unworthy," from *in-* "not, opposite of" + *dignus* "worthy"

WHAT WE THINK OR SAY

"I refuse to be treated in this way. I deserve better."

ITS IMPACT ON OUR OPENNESS TO OTHERS

Closes us

OUR REACTION OR IMPULSE FOR ACTION IS...

To protect myself and my boundaries

RELATED EMOTIONS

Self-respect, self-love

ITS PURPOSE IS TO...

Take care of myself to maintain self-respect

THE TIME ORIENTATION OF THIS EMOTION IS...

Present

HOW THIS EMOTION CAN GET IN THE WAY

Indignation allows us to set and keep personal boundaries. If those boundaries are very large (for instance, in terms of personal space), we may become indignant, to the surprise of others who have different boundaries.

EMOTIONS WE CONFUSE IT WITH

Anger. Indignation is the emotion that allows me to defend the boundaries I've chosen, whereas anger is the emotion in which I want to punish the source of injustice. One is about taking care of me, the other is about punishing another.

HOW IT FEELS OR MOVES US

We protect our legitimacy.

HOW OUR BODY MIGHT FEEL

Energized, heated, focused

HOW OUR BREATH MIGHT BE

Up in the chest, more rapid than at a resting rate, not as fast as in anger

HOW OUR BODY MIGHT SHAPE ITSELF

Stiff, rigid, upright, head tilted up

QUOTE

"A good indignation brings out all one's powers."
—Ralph Waldo Emerson

INFATUATION

ETYMOLOGICAL ROOT

From Latin *infatuare*, "make a fool of," from *in-* "in" + *fatuus* "foolish"

WHAT WE THINK OR SAY

"I know I'm making a fool of myself over him/her, but I don't care."

ITS IMPACT ON OUR OPENNESS TO OTHERS

Opens us

OUR REACTION OR IMPULSE FOR ACTION IS...

To pursue

RELATED EMOTIONS

Admiration, attraction, desire

ITS PURPOSE IS TO...

Let us pursue who or what we want without regard to how we look doing it

THE TIME ORIENTATION OF THIS EMOTION IS...

Present

HOW THIS EMOTION CAN GET IN THE WAY

Infatuation is attraction out of control. It is the emotion in which we often make a fool of ourselves pursuing another person or object.

EMOTIONS WE CONFUSE IT WITH

Attraction. Attraction is the desire to be closer to another; infatuation is doing so in a way that may appear foolish or excessive.

HOW IT FEELS OR MOVES US

Wildly pursuing the object of our infatuation

HOW OUR BODY MIGHT FEEL

Warm

HOW OUR BREATH MIGHT BE

Fast-paced, short, high in the chest

HOW OUR BODY MIGHT SHAPE ITSELF

Open chest and arms, eyes wide

QUOTE

"Violence isn't always evil. What's evil is the infatuation with violence."—*Jim Morrison*

INSPIRATION

ETYMOLOGICAL ROOT

Latin from *in-* "in" + *spirare* "to breathe"

WHAT WE THINK OR SAY

"I'm moved to create."

ITS IMPACT ON OUR OPENNESS TO OTHERS

Opens us

OUR REACTION OR IMPULSE FOR ACTION IS...

To act in new ways

RELATED EMOTIONS

Wonder, enthusiasm

ITS PURPOSE IS TO...

Provoke creativity

THE TIME ORIENTATION OF THIS EMOTION IS...

Future

HOW THIS EMOTION CAN GET IN THE WAY

To be constantly inspired may make it difficult to take action or to value the actions others take.

EMOTIONS WE CONFUSE IT WITH

Enthusiasm. Inspiration comes from the root of "inhale" and is the somatic reaction to a thought or idea which is at the root of creating. Enthusiasm is connection with a greater purpose or mission, and sustains the energy of creation.

HOW IT FEELS OR MOVES US

To dream big dreams and pursue them

HOW OUR BODY MIGHT FEEL

Tingling, flushed

HOW OUR BREATH MIGHT BE

Long, slow, strong deep breathing

HOW OUR BODY MIGHT SHAPE ITSELF

Arms open, head up, chin up, eyes wide

QUOTE

"It is during our darkest moments that we must focus to see the light."—Aristotle

INTRIGUE

ETYMOLOGICAL ROOT

From Latin *intricatus*, "entangled," and *intricare*, "to entangle, perplex, embarrass"

WHAT WE THINK OR SAY

"I'm very interested to know more."

ITS IMPACT ON OUR OPENNESS TO OTHERS

Opens us

OUR REACTION OR IMPULSE FOR ACTION IS...

To investigate

RELATED EMOTIONS

Curiosity, fascination

ITS PURPOSE IS TO...

Untangle complicated situations

THE TIME ORIENTATION OF THIS EMOTION IS...

Present

194

HOW THIS EMOTION CAN GET IN THE WAY

There are people who live for intrigue, which means that they can sometimes become easily bored or disappointed.

EMOTIONS WE CONFUSE IT WITH

Fascination. Intrigue means to "get entangled" in an idea or relationship. Fascination is being enchanted by an idea or relationship.

HOW IT FEELS OR MOVES US

To ask questions, do research, and reflect on new ways of doing things

HOW OUR BODY MIGHT FEEL

Energized

HOW OUR BREATH MIGHT BE

Deeper, longer

HOW OUR BODY MIGHT SHAPE ITSELF

Leaning forward; length, width, and depth are full

QUOTE

"I'm intrigued by fanatics—people who are seduced by the promise, or the illusion, of the absolute."—Jon Krakauer

IRE (IRRITATION)

ETYMOLOGICAL ROOT

From Latin *ira*, "anger, wrath, rage, passion"

WHAT WE THINK OR SAY

"This is bothersome."

ITS IMPACT ON OUR OPENNESS TO OTHERS

Closes us

OUR REACTION OR IMPULSE FOR ACTION IS...

To get rid of or finish as quickly as possible

RELATED EMOTIONS

Anger, aggravation, frustration

ITS PURPOSE IS TO...

Inform us what things are not tolerable

THE TIME ORIENTATION OF THIS EMOTION IS...

Present

HOW THIS EMOTION CAN GET IN THE WAY

Often when we feel irritated, we alienate those around us due to our grumpiness or blaming. It can be very helpful to know what we can tolerate and what we can't, but sometimes it comes with a cost.

EMOTIONS WE CONFUSE IT WITH

Frustration. Ire is the emotion that comes from our passions being provoked, whereas frustration is the belief that things are taking too long or are too complicated.

HOW IT FEELS OR MOVES US

We feel unsettled and want to break free.

HOW OUR BODY MIGHT FEEL

Tense

HOW OUR BREATH MIGHT BE

Shallow, fast

HOW OUR BODY MIGHT SHAPE ITSELF

Jaw tight, belly tight, lack of ground

QUOTE

"The one who cannot restrain their anger will wish undone, what their temper and irritation prompted them to do."—Horace

IRREVERENCE

ETYMOLOGICAL ROOT

Latin *irreverentia*, "want of reverence," from *revereri*, "to stand in awe of, respect, honor, fear, be afraid of"

WHAT WE THINK OR SAY

"I can make light of this even though it is a serious topic."

ITS IMPACT ON OUR OPENNESS TO OTHERS

Opens us

OUR REACTION OR IMPULSE FOR ACTION IS...

To mock or take lightly

RELATED EMOTIONS

Mischievousness, rebelliousness, contempt

ITS PURPOSE IS TO...

Let us be lighthearted even in serious matters

THE TIME ORIENTATION OF THIS EMOTION IS...

Present

HOW THIS EMOTION CAN GET IN THE WAY

Irreverence, like mischievousness, can help us challenge or break out of traditions, but can also alienate us from others who adhere to those traditions.

EMOTIONS WE CONFUSE IT WITH

Disrespect. Irreverence is not to allow the importance of a person or institution to intimidate us, whereas disrespect is to dismiss the legitimacy of a person or institution.

HOW IT FEELS OR MOVES US

We poke fun at or reveal the irony of serious beliefs.

HOW OUR BODY MIGHT FEEL

Light

HOW OUR BREATH MIGHT BE

Quick, shallow

HOW OUR BODY MIGHT SHAPE ITSELF

Tendency to move up and forward, open chest

QUOTE

"Irreverence is the champion of liberty and its only sure defense."—*Mark Twain*

JEALOUSY

ETYMOLOGICAL ROOT

From Latin *zelus*, "zeal," from Greek *zelos*, which sometimes meant "jealousy" but more often was used in a good sense, "emulation, rivalry, zeal"

WHAT WE THINK OR SAY

"I'm afraid I'll lose him/her."

ITS IMPACT ON OUR OPENNESS TO OTHERS

Closes us

OUR REACTION OR IMPULSE FOR ACTION IS...

To hold on to my relationships

RELATED EMOTIONS

Fear, anxiety, envy

ITS PURPOSE IS TO...

Focus our attention on the quality of our relationships and their need for attention

THE TIME ORIENTATION OF THIS EMOTION IS...

Future

HOW THIS EMOTION CAN GET IN THE WAY

Jealousy can get in the way of relationships because our impulse is to hold on more tightly to someone we are afraid of losing connection with. The result is that the other person may feel smothered or suspected of wrongdoing.

EMOTIONS WE CONFUSE IT WITH

Envy. Envy is the desire to have something in our life that we see others have in theirs, whether it is material or immaterial. Jealousy is the fear that we will lose a relationship or connection that is important to us.

HOW IT FEELS OR MOVES US

Brings our attention to a relationship out of fear of losing it

HOW OUR BODY MIGHT FEEL

Tight in the belly, chest, and shoulders

HOW OUR BREATH MIGHT BE

Fairly rapid, high in the chest

HOW OUR BODY MIGHT SHAPE ITSELF

Eyes narrowed, chest closed but not collapsed

QUOTE

"Jealousy lives upon doubts. It becomes madness or ceases entirely as soon as we pass from doubt to certainty."
—Francois de La Rochefoucauld

JOY

The emotion is.............................

ETYMOLOGICAL ROOT

From Latin *gaudia*, "feeling of pleasure and delight"

WHAT WE THINK OR SAY

"Let's celebrate."

ITS IMPACT ON OUR OPENNESS TO OTHERS

Opens us

OUR REACTION OR IMPULSE FOR ACTION IS...

To celebrate

RELATED EMOTIONS

Delight, happiness

ITS PURPOSE IS TO...

Let us celebrate

THE TIME ORIENTATION OF THIS EMOTION IS...

Present

HOW THIS EMOTION CAN GET IN THE WAY

Unmitigated joy would be a kind of euphoria and could lead to disconnection with the day-to-day needs of life.

EMOTIONS WE CONFUSE IT WITH

Happiness. Joy means we believe life is worth celebrating. Happiness means we like how life is turning out.

HOW IT FEELS OR MOVES US

We feel like celebrating and expressing our joy.

HOW OUR BODY MIGHT FEEL

Elevated, energy flowing through your body

HOW OUR BREATH MIGHT BE

Deep, even

HOW OUR BODY MIGHT SHAPE ITSELF

Arms wide in a 'V,' head and chin up, smiling

QUOTE

"When you rise in the morning, give thanks for the light, for your life, for your strength. Give thanks for the joy of living. If you see no reason to give thanks, the fault lies in yourself."—Tecumseh

KINDNESS

ETYMOLOGICAL ROOT

From Old English *gecynde*, "natural, native, innate," originally "with the feeling of relatives for each other"

WHAT WE THINK OR SAY

"I feel like one of the family."

ITS IMPACT ON OUR OPENNESS TO OTHERS

Opens us

OUR REACTION OR IMPULSE FOR ACTION IS...

To welcome

RELATED EMOTIONS

Compassion, attraction, tenderness

ITS PURPOSE IS TO...

Let us be welcoming and inclusive of others

THE TIME ORIENTATION OF THIS EMOTION IS...

Present

HOW THIS EMOTION CAN GET IN THE WAY

Kindness is universally considered a good emotion, and we are encouraged to extend it to strangers. It opens connections but can make one vulnerable if the intention of the other is to take advantage.

EMOTIONS WE CONFUSE IT WITH

Compassion. Kindness means we treat people as we would a relative (or at least those relatives we like), whereas compassion means we can be present with another person but retain our own emotion and center.

HOW IT FEELS OR MOVES US

We treat others well.

HOW OUR BODY MIGHT FEEL

Relaxed, inclined to move towards

HOW OUR BREATH MIGHT BE

Slow, regular, deep

HOW OUR BODY MIGHT SHAPE ITSELF

Open, arms reaching out, smile

QUOTE

"No act of kindness, no matter how small, is ever wasted."—Aesop

LASCIVIOUSNESS

ETYMOLOGICAL ROOT

From Late Latin *lascivia*, "lewdness, playfulness, frolicsomeness, jollity"

WHAT WE THINK OR SAY

"I feel like doing lewd and wicked things."

ITS IMPACT ON OUR OPENNESS TO OTHERS

Opens us

OUR REACTION OR IMPULSE FOR ACTION IS...

To flirt

RELATED EMOTIONS

Lust, passion, desire, eroticism

ITS PURPOSE IS TO...

Connect sexually or erotically

THE TIME ORIENTATION OF THIS EMOTION IS...

Present

HOW THIS EMOTION CAN GET IN THE WAY

Lasciviousness is intensely focused on sexual pleasure and is thus one dimension in a world of many dimensions. A focus here, when not shared by the other person, is generally seen as inappropriate or abusive.

EMOTIONS WE CONFUSE IT WITH

Lust. Lasciviousness means to be playful in a lewd or sexual way. Lust is the desire "to have" no matter what the consequences and can apply to any aspect of life, not just sex.

HOW IT FEELS OR MOVES US

To pursue sexual or erotic connection

HOW OUR BODY MIGHT FEEL

Energized, tingling

HOW OUR BREATH MIGHT BE

Moderately paced, middle chest

HOW OUR BODY MIGHT SHAPE ITSELF

Open, tendency to move up and back

QUOTE

"Well, I will find you twenty lascivious turtles ere one chaste man."—William Shakespeare

207

LAZINESS

ETYMOLOGICAL ROOT

Probably comes from Low German *laisch*, "weak, feeble, tired"

WHAT WE THINK OR SAY

"I don't feel like doing much of anything."

ITS IMPACT ON OUR OPENNESS TO OTHERS

Neutral

OUR REACTION OR IMPULSE FOR ACTION IS...

Do little or nothing

RELATED EMOTIONS

Calmness, resignation, boredom, indifference

ITS PURPOSE IS TO...

Rest, recuperate, and enjoy doing nothing

THE TIME ORIENTATION OF THIS EMOTION IS...

Present

HOW THIS EMOTION CAN GET IN THE WAY

Laziness has long been maligned as a bad emotion. It has been consider as "leading to no good," and is rarely seen as having value. A mood of laziness does not support action even when needed.

EMOTIONS WE CONFUSE IT WITH

Contentment. In the emotion of laziness we want to rest because we are tired or lack physical energy. Contentment is to rest because we are satisfied with the conditions as they are and do not feel a need to change them.

HOW IT FEELS OR MOVES US

To do as little as possible

HOW OUR BODY MIGHT FEEL

Slack, loose, relaxed

HOW OUR BREATH MIGHT BE

Long, slow, shallow

HOW OUR BODY MIGHT SHAPE ITSELF

Tendency to move back and down, open, arms at the side, jaw relaxed, shoulders relaxed

QUOTE

"Laziness is nothing more than the habit of resting before you get tired."—Jules Renard

LONELINESS

ETYMOLOGICAL ROOT

c. 1600, "solitary, solo," from *lone* + *-ly*

WHAT WE THINK OR SAY

"I'm alone and something is missing."

ITS IMPACT ON OUR OPENNESS TO OTHERS

Closes us

OUR REACTION OR IMPULSE FOR ACTION IS...

To seek others for company

RELATED EMOTIONS

Hopelessness, sadness, despair

ITS PURPOSE IS TO...

Urge us to seek out others to complete our sense of self

THE TIME ORIENTATION OF THIS EMOTION IS...

Present

HOW THIS EMOTION CAN GET IN THE WAY

Loneliness is the belief that we are alone and not connected with others which, when maintained, becomes a self-fulfilling belief.

EMOTIONS WE CONFUSE IT WITH

Sadness. Loneliness is the belief that we are alone and others do not or cannot understand our situation. Sadness is the loss of something or someone we care about.

HOW IT FEELS OR MOVES US

To seek company

HOW OUR BODY MIGHT FEEL

Lethargic

HOW OUR BREATH MIGHT BE

Slow, shallow, occasionally deep sighs

HOW OUR BODY MIGHT SHAPE ITSELF

Slumped shoulders, downward energy

"Loneliness expresses the pain of being alone and solitude expresses the glory of being alone."—Paul Tillich

LOVE

The emotion is............................

ETYMOLOGICAL ROOT

Old English *lufian*, "to cherish, show love to; delight in, approve"

WHAT WE THINK OR SAY

"I cherish you just as you are."

ITS IMPACT ON OUR OPENNESS TO OTHERS

Opens us

OUR REACTION OR IMPULSE FOR ACTION IS...

To honor and cherish

RELATED EMOTIONS

Lust, desire, infatuation, adoration

ITS PURPOSE IS TO...

Accept the other as they are

THE TIME ORIENTATION OF THIS EMOTION IS...

Present

HOW THIS EMOTION CAN GET IN THE WAY

Since love is accepting another as legitimate the way they are, we do not have any desire to change them. This could lead to enabling them to remain as they are even if that way of being is not healthy for them.

EMOTIONS WE CONFUSE IT WITH

Passion. Love is the emotion where we hold the other as legitimate just as they are and have no desire to change them. Passion is the desire to become one with another and can apply to experiences as well as people.

HOW IT FEELS OR MOVES US

To work toward acceptance of the other person as they are

HOW OUR BODY MIGHT FEEL

Warm, gentle streaming of energy flowing throughout the body

HOW OUR BREATH MIGHT BE

Slow, consistent, even-paced, abdominal

HOW OUR BODY MIGHT SHAPE ITSELF

Open, head with a slight tilt perhaps, tendency to move up and back, smile

QUOTE

"We are most alive when we're in love."—John Updike

LOYALTY

The emotion is.................

ETYMOLOGICAL ROOT

Latin *legalem*, from *lex* "law"

WHAT WE THINK OR SAY

"I'll defend you; I've got your back."

ITS IMPACT ON OUR OPENNESS TO OTHERS

Closes us

OUR REACTION OR IMPULSE FOR ACTION IS…

To defend a relationship or group I'm part of

RELATED EMOTIONS

Admiration, trust, reverence

ITS PURPOSE IS TO…

Preserve the relationship, group, or community

THE TIME ORIENTATION OF THIS EMOTION IS…

Past, present, or future

HOW THIS EMOTION CAN GET IN THE WAY

Out of loyalty we can sometimes neglect our own values and end up acting in ways we disagree with or loathe.

EMOTIONS WE CONFUSE IT WITH

Trust. Loyalty is the belief that we are part of a group and are willing to defend it. Trust is the belief that we are not taking undue risk coordinating action with another.

HOW IT FEELS OR MOVES US

To defend or take the side of the person or group we are loyal to

HOW OUR BODY MIGHT FEEL

Full, warm, energized

HOW OUR BREATH MIGHT BE

Even, mid-chest

HOW OUR BODY MIGHT SHAPE ITSELF

Depth is expanded

QUOTE

"I'll take fifty percent efficiency to get one hundred percent loyalty."—Samuel Goldwyn

LUST

The emotion is ....

WHAT WE THINK OR SAY

"I want x without regard to the consequences."

ITS IMPACT ON OUR OPENNESS TO OTHERS

Closes us

OUR REACTION OR IMPULSE FOR ACTION IS...

To pursue

RELATED EMOTIONS

Love, infatuation, passion, lasciviousness

ITS PURPOSE IS TO...

Show us what we desire

THE TIME ORIENTATION OF THIS EMOTION IS...

Present

HOW THIS EMOTION CAN GET IN THE WAY

Lust is a hunger that puts us in single-minded pursuit of what we desire, which can lead us to act in ways not aligned with our values or those of our community.

EMOTIONS WE CONFUSE IT WITH

Passion. Lust is the desire to have someone or something regardless of the consequences, whereas passion is the desire to become one with another. Either can apply to people, things, or experiences.

HOW IT FEELS OR MOVES US

We go after whoever or whatever we desire.

HOW OUR BODY MIGHT FEEL

Tingling all over, knot in the pit of the stomach, energized

HOW OUR BREATH MIGHT BE

Fast-paced in the upper chest

HOW OUR BODY MIGHT SHAPE ITSELF

Tendency to move forward and down, eyes focused, chest open

QUOTE

"Let us all be brave enough to die the death of a martyr; but let no one lust for martyrdom."—Mahatma Gandhi

MAGNANIMITY

The emotion

WHAT WE THINK OR SAY

"I want to take care of others in important ways."

ITS IMPACT ON OUR OPENNESS TO OTHERS

Opens us

OUR REACTION OR IMPULSE FOR ACTION IS...

To give generously

RELATED EMOTIONS

Generosity, service

ITS PURPOSE IS TO...

Use our resources for the care of others

THE TIME ORIENTATION OF THIS EMOTION IS...

Future

HOW THIS EMOTION CAN GET IN THE WAY

Magnanimity, although well intentioned, can be seen as arrogance or pity by others.

EMOTIONS WE CONFUSE IT WITH

Generous. Generosity is related to sharing our resources, while magnanimity is more focused on taking care of others or changing circumstances in order for them to be taken care of (e.g., setting up a charitable foundation).

HOW IT FEELS OR MOVES US

To give or take care of others in large or significant ways, often demonstrated at the level of community.

HOW OUR BODY MIGHT FEEL

Warm, gentle flowing energy

HOW OUR BREATH MIGHT BE

Long, slow, deep breaths

HOW OUR BODY MIGHT SHAPE ITSELF

Open, arms reaching out, smile

QUOTE

"If the gentleman has ability, he is magnanimous, generous, tolerant, and straightforward, through which he opens the way to instruct others."—Xun Kuang

MELANCHOLY

ETYMOLOGICAL ROOT

Greek *melankholia*, "sadness," literally (excess of) "black bile"

WHAT WE THINK OR SAY

"I don't feel like doing anything."

ITS IMPACT ON OUR OPENNESS TO OTHERS

Closes us

OUR REACTION OR IMPULSE FOR ACTION IS...

To wallow in listlessness

RELATED EMOTIONS

Sadness, nostalgia, wistfulness, regret

ITS PURPOSE IS TO...

Know when we are out of balance

THE TIME ORIENTATION OF THIS EMOTION IS...

Present

HOW THIS EMOTION CAN GET IN THE WAY

In the intense sadness of melancholy, we often separate ourselves from others and are beyond their reach to help us.

EMOTIONS WE CONFUSE IT WITH

Sadness. Melancholy is the emotion in which we have lost interest in life generally, while sadness signals that we have lost something we care about.

HOW IT FEELS OR MOVES US

To feel sorry for ourselves

HOW OUR BODY MIGHT FEEL

Lack of energy, tendency to move back and down or to stay still

HOW OUR BREATH MIGHT BE

Very shallow, and slow breathing

HOW OUR BODY MIGHT SHAPE ITSELF

Collapsed width, length, and depth

QUOTE

"Melancholy is no bad thing."—Sting

MISCHIEVOUSNESS

ETYMOLOGICAL ROOT

From Old French *meschief*, "misfortune, harm, trouble; annoyance, vexation"

WHAT WE THINK OR SAY

"I know it is a little naughty, but I'm going to do it anyway."

ITS IMPACT ON OUR OPENNESS TO OTHERS

Can open or close us

OUR REACTION OR IMPULSE FOR ACTION IS…

To provoke in a playful way

RELATED EMOTIONS

Irreverence, disrespect

ITS PURPOSE IS TO…

Play at provoking others

THE TIME ORIENTATION OF THIS EMOTION IS…

Present

HOW THIS EMOTION CAN GET IN THE WAY

We can be playful and provocative when mischievous, but we can also alienate and mock or diminish others. Balance is crucial.

EMOTIONS WE CONFUSE IT WITH

Vengeance. To be mischievous is to be intentionally and playfully annoying, while vengeance is the desire to get even for a past injustice or unfairness.

HOW IT FEELS OR MOVES US

To tease, mock, or provoke others in a playful way

HOW OUR BODY MIGHT FEEL

Energized, tendency to move upward and forward

HOW OUR BREATH MIGHT BE

High in the chest, fast-paced

HOW OUR BODY MIGHT SHAPE ITSELF

Elongated length, slight smile, bright eyes

QUOTE

"We all want to be a little glamorous, a little playful, and a little mischievous at times."—Jason Wu

MISERY

ETYMOLOGICAL ROOT

From Latin *miseria*, "wretchedness"

WHAT WE THINK OR SAY

"Life is bad."

ITS IMPACT ON OUR OPENNESS TO OTHERS

Closes us

OUR REACTION OR IMPULSE FOR ACTION IS...

To suffer

RELATED EMOTIONS

Anguish, sadness, hopelessness

ITS PURPOSE IS TO...

Let us see how unpleasant life can be

THE TIME ORIENTATION OF THIS EMOTION IS...

Present

HOW THIS EMOTION CAN GET IN THE WAY

To feel misery is to collapse and suffer. It may be true that "misery loves company," but that company does not help us move out of misery.

EMOTIONS WE CONFUSE IT WITH

Despair. Despair means loss of hope, whereas misery means our current life is bad or very difficult.

HOW IT FEELS OR MOVES US

We feel self-pity and sorry for ourselves.

HOW OUR BODY MIGHT FEEL

Very heavy, sluggish

HOW OUR BREATH MIGHT BE

Short, shallow breaths

HOW OUR BODY MIGHT SHAPE ITSELF

Fully collapsed into itself

QUOTE

"Extreme hopes are born from extreme misery."
—Bertrand Russell

MODESTY

ETYMOLOGICAL ROOT

From Latin *modestus*, "keeping due measure"

WHAT WE THINK OR SAY

"I'm behaving in a proper way."

ITS IMPACT ON OUR OPENNESS TO OTHERS

Can open or close us

OUR REACTION OR IMPULSE FOR ACTION IS...

To act properly

RELATED EMOTIONS

Prudence, shyness, caution

ITS PURPOSE IS TO...

Let us behave in ways that preserve our place in a community

THE TIME ORIENTATION OF THIS EMOTION IS...

Present

226

HOW THIS EMOTION CAN GET IN THE WAY

Living a quiet and contained life has its benefits, but modesty can keep us from being bold or trying things we regard as extreme.

EMOTIONS WE CONFUSE IT WITH

Timidity. Modesty is the desire to do things in an acceptable fashion and to avoid extremes. Timidity is the desire to act in a way that avoids attention.

HOW IT FEELS OR MOVES US

To avoid extremes in our thoughts and actions

HOW OUR BODY MIGHT FEEL

Relaxed, calm

HOW OUR BREATH MIGHT BE

Breath is even and slow

HOW OUR BODY MIGHT SHAPE ITSELF

Open, perhaps a slight diminishment in width, not wanting to take up too much space.

QUOTE

"Let us be absolutely clear about one thing: we must not confuse humility with false modesty or servility."
—*Paulo Coelho*

MORTIFICATION

ETYMOLOGICAL ROOT

From Late Latin *mortificare*, "cause death, kill, put to death," literally "make dead"

WHAT WE THINK OR SAY

"I want to crawl in a hole and die."

ITS IMPACT ON OUR OPENNESS TO OTHERS

Closes us

OUR REACTION OR IMPULSE FOR ACTION IS...

To hide or want to disappear

RELATED EMOTIONS

Embarrassment, shame, guilt

ITS PURPOSE IS TO...

Preserve our personal identity

THE TIME ORIENTATION OF THIS EMOTION IS...

Past

HOW THIS EMOTION CAN GET IN THE WAY

To feel mortified is to have the sensation of being "dead while still living." It separates us from life and other people due to our belief we have done something bad enough to deserve dying.

EMOTIONS WE CONFUSE IT WITH

Embarrassment. Mortified means we feel we would rather die than have people know about something we've done, whereas being embarrassed is only that we'd like to avoid people knowing what we've done.

HOW IT FEELS OR MOVES US

To withdraw and hope others won't see us

HOW OUR BODY MIGHT FEEL

Tight

HOW OUR BREATH MIGHT BE

Short and shallow

HOW OUR BODY MIGHT SHAPE ITSELF

Length shortened, depth collapsed, and width diminished, head down

QUOTE

"I went hunting, I shot a deer, and it mortified me. I just couldn't do it again."—*Channing Tatum*

NAÏVETÉ

ETYMOLOGICAL ROOT

From Latin *nativus*, "not artificial," also "native, rustic," literally "born, innate, natural"

WHAT WE THINK OR SAY

"The world should be the way I want it to be."

OUR REACTION OR IMPULSE FOR ACTION IS...

To ignore what is unpleasant

ITS PURPOSE IS TO...

Proceed in ignorance of things that might constrain us

ITS IMPACT ON OUR OPENNESS TO OTHERS

Opens us

RELATED EMOTIONS

Denial, infatuation, loyalty

THE TIME ORIENTATION OF THIS EMOTION IS...

Future

HOW THIS EMOTION CAN GET IN THE WAY

Naïveté produces blindness to things we'd rather not see. It keeps us from seeing the world as it is because we are only willing to look at what we consider "good."

EMOTIONS WE CONFUSE IT WITH

Entitlement. In naïveté we believe the world should match our ideal, whereas in entitlement we believe the world owes us a certain status, relationships, or material objects.

HOW IT FEELS OR MOVES US

It blinds us to things we would rather not know about

HOW OUR BODY MIGHT FEEL

Relaxed and open

HOW OUR BREATH MIGHT BE

Slow, even, medium depth

HOW OUR BODY MIGHT SHAPE ITSELF

Excess length with a lack of groundedness

QUOTE

"It was my delusion and naïveté that brought me here."
—*Lady Gaga*

231

NOSTALGIA

ETYMOLOGICAL ROOT

From Greek *algos*, "pain, grief, distress" + *nostos*, "homecoming"

WHAT WE THINK OR SAY

"The past was better than the present, and I'd like to go back."

ITS IMPACT ON OUR OPENNESS TO OTHERS

Closes us

OUR REACTION OR IMPULSE FOR ACTION IS...

To yearn for the past

RELATED EMOTIONS

Wistfulness, sentimentality, yearning

ITS PURPOSE IS TO...

Know how good life can be from previous experience

THE TIME ORIENTATION OF THIS EMOTION IS...

Past

232

HOW THIS EMOTION CAN GET IN THE WAY

Looking back to when times were better can become a way of living or a mood. When it does, we will spend our time longing or yearning for the past rather than trying to bring forward the elements we appreciated from that time.

EMOTIONS WE CONFUSE IT WITH

Regret. Nostalgia is the belief that "life was better in the past" and we have a desire to re-create it. Regret is the belief that "life today would be better if we had/had not done something in the past."

HOW IT FEELS OR MOVES US

To look back longingly at life as we remember it being

HOW OUR BODY MIGHT FEEL

Somewhat heavy

HOW OUR BREATH MIGHT BE

Slow, belly breathing

HOW OUR BODY MIGHT SHAPE ITSELF

Depth is expanded, length somewhat diminished

QUOTE

"Nostalgia isn't what it used to be."—Peter De Vries

OBLIGATION

ETYMOLOGICAL ROOT

From Latin *obligare*, "to bind, bind up, bandage"

WHAT WE THINK OR SAY

"I have no choice."

ITS IMPACT ON OUR OPENNESS TO OTHERS

Closes us

OUR REACTION OR IMPULSE FOR ACTION IS...

To do my duty

RELATED EMOTIONS

Loyalty, obsequity, resignation

ITS PURPOSE IS TO...

Tell us what we must do

THE TIME ORIENTATION OF THIS EMOTION IS...

Present

HOW THIS EMOTION CAN GET IN THE WAY

Sometimes we believe we are obligated when in fact we are only acting out of habit. True obligation allows us to do what we must, but questioning the source and truthfulness of the obligation is a good practice.

EMOTIONS WE CONFUSE IT WITH

Responsibility. Obligation is the belief that we have no choice except to act in a particular way, whereas responsibility is the belief that our public identity depends on us doing things in a particular way.

HOW IT FEELS OR MOVES US

We do our duty because we believe we have no other choice.

HOW OUR BODY MIGHT FEEL

Weighed down

HOW OUR BREATH MIGHT BE

Slow, shallow

HOW OUR BODY MIGHT SHAPE ITSELF

Shoulders slumped, chest concave

QUOTE

"The Universe is under no obligation to make sense to you."—Neil deGrasse Tyson

OBSEQUIOUSNESS

WHAT WE THINK OR SAY

"I must obey."

ITS IMPACT ON OUR OPENNESS TO OTHERS

Closes us

OUR REACTION OR IMPULSE FOR ACTION IS...

To try to please

RELATED EMOTIONS

Humility, fear, modesty

ITS PURPOSE IS TO...

Allow us to submit

THE TIME ORIENTATION OF THIS EMOTION IS...

Present

HOW THIS EMOTION CAN GET IN THE WAY

Obsequity or putting ourselves below others has obvious negative consequences. It can be essential for survival in some situations, but may create a sustained belief we are not as important as other people.

EMOTIONS WE CONFUSE IT WITH

Humility. Obsequiousness is the emotion in which we see ourselves as less important than others. Humility means we claim all that we are but nothing we are not and is a way of maintaining perspective on our place in the world.

HOW IT FEELS OR MOVES US

We feel less important than others and therefore respond to their demands.

HOW OUR BODY MIGHT FEEL

Tight in the throat

HOW OUR BREATH MIGHT BE

High-paced, and high in the chest

HOW OUR BODY MIGHT SHAPE ITSELF

Length and width diminished significantly

QUOTE

"You have to take your ego out of it and say, 'Do I want people to be obsequious to me or do I want to write good books?' If it's the latter, you have to take criticism. It's annoying, but that's how to do good stuff; listen to other people."—Denise Mina

237

OPTIMISM

ETYMOLOGICAL ROOT

From Latin *optimus*, "the best"

WHAT WE THINK OR SAY

"I know good things and bad things happen to people, but mostly good things happen to me."

ITS IMPACT ON OUR OPENNESS TO OTHERS

Opens us

OUR REACTION OR IMPULSE FOR ACTION IS...

To act freely with hope for a good outcome

RELATED EMOTIONS

Hope, ambition, enthusiasm

ITS PURPOSE IS TO...

Keep us looking for the silver lining in all things

THE TIME ORIENTATION OF THIS EMOTION IS...

Future

HOW THIS EMOTION CAN GET IN THE WAY

Most people see optimism as a "good" emotion, but if it does not allow us to be grounded or realistic, it can blind us to danger.

EMOTIONS WE CONFUSE IT WITH

Hope. Optimism means I recognize that good and bad things happen to people, but mostly good things happen to me. Hope is the belief that life in the future will be an improvement over what it is now or was in the past.

HOW IT FEELS OR MOVES US

We act confidently, believing the outcome will be good.

HOW OUR BODY MIGHT FEEL

Energized

HOW OUR BREATH MIGHT BE

Fast-paced, mid-chest

HOW OUR BODY MIGHT SHAPE ITSELF

Open and moving forward

QUOTE

"Optimism is the madness of insisting that all is well when we are miserable."—*Voltaire*

PANIC

ETYMOLOGICAL ROOT

From Greek *panikon*, literally "pertaining to Pan," the god of woods and fields, who was the source of mysterious sounds that caused contagious, groundless fear in herds and crowds, or in people in lonely spots

WHAT WE THINK OR SAY

"I need to get away."

ITS IMPACT ON OUR OPENNESS TO OTHERS

Closes us

OUR REACTION OR IMPULSE FOR ACTION IS...

To run

RELATED EMOTIONS

Urgency, fear, terror

ITS PURPOSE IS TO...

Flee danger

THE TIME ORIENTATION OF THIS EMOTION IS...

Present

HOW THIS EMOTION CAN GET IN THE WAY

Panic is essential when we find ourselves in a dangerous or threatening situation. However, frequent or constant panic will exhaust us.

EMOTIONS WE CONFUSE IT WITH

Urgency. Panic is the emotion that provokes us to act immediately, but sometimes without clear direction. Urgency comes from the root "to press hard" and means to proceed with focus and intensity.

HOW IT FEELS OR MOVES US

We feel an urgency to get away or resolve a crisis immediately.

HOW OUR BODY MIGHT FEEL

Lots of energy streaming through it

HOW OUR BREATH MIGHT BE

Very high in the chest, very fast-paced

HOW OUR BODY MIGHT SHAPE ITSELF

Eyes narrow, loss of peripheral vision, wild, erratic movements

QUOTE

"DON'T PANIC."—Douglas Adams

241

PARANOIA

ETYMOLOGICAL ROOT

From Greek *paranoia*, "mental derangement, madness," from *paranoos*, "mentally ill, insane," from *para-* "beside, beyond" + *noos* "mind"

WHAT WE THINK OR SAY

"Everyone or everything is trying to harm me."

ITS IMPACT ON OUR OPENNESS TO OTHERS

Closes us

OUR REACTION OR IMPULSE FOR ACTION IS...

To fear the intentions of other people

RELATED EMOTIONS

Fear, anxiety, dread

ITS PURPOSE IS TO...

Keep us safe from others who may want to harm us

THE TIME ORIENTATION OF THIS EMOTION IS...

Future

HOW THIS EMOTION CAN GET IN THE WAY

Paranoia tries to keep us safe from others who might harm us. Its hypervigilance keeps us from ever resting, and ultimately that may be more damaging than any threat from other people.

EMOTIONS WE CONFUSE IT WITH

Fear. Fear is the belief that something specific may harm us, but it could include many possibilities; paranoia is the belief that other people or the world more generally is plotting to do us harm.

HOW IT FEELS OR MOVES US

To be hypervigilant and not allow others to get close

HOW OUR BODY MIGHT FEEL

Tight

HOW OUR BREATH MIGHT BE

Fast in upper chest

HOW OUR BODY MIGHT SHAPE ITSELF

Eyes darting and narrow, head down, length, width, and depth all diminished

QUOTE

"There is no such thing as paranoia. Your worst fears can come true at any moment."—Hunter S. Thompson

PASSION

ETYMOLOGICAL ROOT

From Late Latin *passionem*, "suffering, enduring"

WHAT WE THINK OR SAY

"I have a deep desire to be a part of x."

ITS IMPACT ON OUR OPENNESS TO OTHERS

Opens us

OUR REACTION OR IMPULSE FOR ACTION IS...

To be as close as possible

RELATED EMOTIONS

Desire, love, lust, infatuation

ITS PURPOSE IS TO...

Produce intimacy

THE TIME ORIENTATION OF THIS EMOTION IS...

Present

HOW THIS EMOTION CAN GET IN THE WAY

Passion is full engagement, but only in one thing. Being fully engaged with one thing or person means we cannot be engaged with others. In that sense, it can interfere with living a balanced life.

EMOTIONS WE CONFUSE IT WITH

Desire. Passion has to do with sharing in the deepest way possible, even when it is filled with pain. Desire is the hope for something to become part of your life.

HOW IT FEELS OR MOVES US

To get close to a person or engage in something we long to be a part of

HOW OUR BODY MIGHT FEEL

Very energized and invigorated

HOW OUR BREATH MIGHT BE

Long, deep, fast breathing

HOW OUR BODY MIGHT SHAPE ITSELF

Arms wide open, eyes and mouth wide open, length and width and depth full

QUOTE

"Great dancers are not great because of their technique, they are great because of their passion."—Martha Graham

PATIENCE

ETYMOLOGICAL ROOT

Latin *patientia*, "endurance, submission, indulgence, leniency."
Literally "quality of suffering"

WHAT WE THINK OR SAY

"I can wait."

ITS IMPACT ON OUR OPENNESS TO OTHERS

Opens us

OUR REACTION OR IMPULSE FOR ACTION IS...

To wait

RELATED EMOTIONS

Tolerance, acceptance, calmness

ITS PURPOSE IS TO...

Allow us to adjust to the rhythm of others

THE TIME ORIENTATION OF THIS EMOTION IS...

Present

HOW THIS EMOTION CAN GET IN THE WAY

Patience, when it is not warranted, can be dangerous. It can also allow us to betray our standards and sacrifice our dignity.

EMOTIONS WE CONFUSE IT WITH

Tolerance. Patience means "I'm willing to wait until everything is ready to move forward." Tolerance means "I'll put up with the current situation until it changes."

HOW IT FEELS OR MOVES US

To wait for others to be ready as we are

HOW OUR BODY MIGHT FEEL

Relaxed and calm

HOW OUR BREATH MIGHT BE

Long, slow, deep breaths

HOW OUR BODY MIGHT SHAPE ITSELF

Head slightly tilted to the side or down; length, width, and depth are balanced

QUOTE

"We could never learn to be brave and patient if there were only joy in the world."—Helen Keller

PEACE

The emotion is.......................

ETYMOLOGICAL ROOT

From Latin *pacem*, "compact, agreement, treaty of peace, tranquility, absence of war"

WHAT WE THINK OR SAY

"All is well."

ITS IMPACT ON OUR OPENNESS TO OTHERS

Opens us

OUR REACTION OR IMPULSE FOR ACTION IS...

To rest

RELATED EMOTIONS

Serenity, acceptance, calmness

ITS PURPOSE IS TO...

Rest without worry

THE TIME ORIENTATION OF THIS EMOTION IS...

Present

HOW THIS EMOTION CAN GET IN THE WAY

Peace is a blessing in a world that is constantly on the move, but if we were permanently in peace, we could find ourselves bored and disengaged from the world.

EMOTIONS WE CONFUSE IT WITH

Serenity. Peace is the absence of conflict, hence we are aware that conflict still exists. Serenity is the belief that all is calm and there is no conflict to be aware of.

HOW IT FEELS OR MOVES US

We feel very calm and at ease.

HOW OUR BODY MIGHT FEEL

Relaxed and calm

HOW OUR BREATH MIGHT BE

Slow deep breath

HOW OUR BODY MIGHT SHAPE ITSELF

Open

QUOTE

"Peace is its own reward."—Mahatma Gandhi

PERSEVERANCE

ETYMOLOGICAL ROOT

From Latin *perseverantia*, "steadfastness, constancy"

WHAT WE THINK OR SAY

"I'll continue trying until I succeed."

ITS IMPACT ON OUR OPENNESS TO OTHERS

Can open or close us

OUR REACTION OR IMPULSE FOR ACTION IS...

To keep trying

RELATED EMOTIONS

Enthusiasm, obligation, passion

ITS PURPOSE IS TO...

Continue trying until we succeed

THE TIME ORIENTATION OF THIS EMOTION IS...

Future

HOW THIS EMOTION CAN GET IN THE WAY

The expression "hitting my head against the wall because it feels so good to stop" encapsulates the way perseverance can get in our way. It is useful when balanced with awareness of when to accept or surrender to the situation.

EMOTIONS WE CONFUSE IT WITH

Stubbornness. Perseverance is the energy to continue trying even though results are not visible. Stubbornness is an unwillingness to change.

HOW IT FEELS OR MOVES US

To push forward and look for new ways to succeed

HOW OUR BODY MIGHT FEEL

Strong, grounded, moving forward

HOW OUR BREATH MIGHT BE

Even, slow, and steady

HOW OUR BODY MIGHT SHAPE ITSELF

Moving forward and down

QUOTE

"Great works are performed not by strength but by perseverance."—Samuel Johnson

PESSIMISM

ETYMOLOGICAL ROOT

Latin *pessimus*, "worst," originally "bottommost"

WHAT WE THINK OR SAY

"I know good things and bad things happen to people, but mostly bad things happen to me."

ITS IMPACT ON OUR OPENNESS TO OTHERS

Closes us

OUR REACTION OR IMPULSE FOR ACTION IS...

To act reluctantly

RELATED EMOTIONS

Skepticism, cynicism, resignation

ITS PURPOSE IS TO...

Let us live with minimal expectations

THE TIME ORIENTATION OF THIS EMOTION IS...

Future

HOW THIS EMOTION CAN GET IN THE WAY

When pessimism becomes resignation, it quits being a useful emotion. If we understand it as "good things and bad things happen to people, but mostly bad things happen to me," we can look for the source or cause of those things to rectify them.

EMOTIONS WE CONFUSE IT WITH

Skepticism. Pessimism is the belief that good things and bad things happen to people, but that mostly bad things happen to me. Skepticism occurs when we are trying to determine whether to retain a former belief or to believe something newly encountered.

HOW IT FEELS OR MOVES US

We tend to act with little energy or commitment.

HOW OUR BODY MIGHT FEEL

Somewhat tense in the shoulders and neck

HOW OUR BREATH MIGHT BE

Short and shallow

HOW OUR BODY MIGHT SHAPE ITSELF

Looking down, length diminished somewhat

QUOTE

"My pessimism extends to the point of even suspecting the sincerity of other pessimists."—Jean Rostand

PITY

ETYMOLOGICAL ROOT

Early 13c., from Old French *pite*, *pitet*, "pity, mercy, compassion, care, tenderness; wretched condition"

WHAT WE THINK OR SAY

"I'm aware of others' suffering, but feel superior because I believe it is their own fault."

ITS IMPACT ON OUR OPENNESS TO OTHERS

Closes us

OUR REACTION OR IMPULSE FOR ACTION IS...

To look down on another

RELATED EMOTIONS

Empathy, sympathy, compassion

ITS PURPOSE IS TO...

Help others who need our support

THE TIME ORIENTATION OF THIS EMOTION IS...

Present

HOW THIS EMOTION CAN GET IN THE WAY

Pity can be confused with compassion, sympathy, or empathy, and has the quality of "superiority" about it. There are moments that is accurate and important, but in other situations it appears arrogant and condescending.

EMOTIONS WE CONFUSE IT WITH

Compassion. Pity means "this person or thing needs my help because I have a superior ability," whereas compassion is the ability to help someone from the emotion I choose while remaining on an equal level.

HOW IT FEELS OR MOVES US

To help others we consider less fortunate

HOW OUR BODY MIGHT FEEL

Downward energy, slow

HOW OUR BREATH MIGHT BE

Very slow into the mid-chest (heart) region

HOW OUR BODY MIGHT SHAPE ITSELF

Head down, shoulders rounded

QUOTE

"Pity and friendship are two passions incompatible with each other."—Oliver Goldsmith

PRIDE

ETYMOLOGICAL ROOT

From Late Latin *prode*, "advantageous, profitable," Old English mid-12c. in the reflexive sense "congratulate (oneself), be proud"

WHAT WE THINK OR SAY

"I did something good and want others to know."

ITS IMPACT ON OUR OPENNESS TO OTHERS

Opens us

OUR REACTION OR IMPULSE FOR ACTION IS…

To tell others what I have done

RELATED EMOTIONS

Arrogance, happiness

ITS PURPOSE IS TO…

Share what we've done in order to receive recognition from others

THE TIME ORIENTATION OF THIS EMOTION IS…

Past

HOW THIS EMOTION CAN GET IN THE WAY

Excessive pride would show up in continually telling others about all the wonderful things we've done. As an emotion that allows us to share, it is helpful; as an emotion that allows us to dominate, it is not.

EMOTIONS WE CONFUSE IT WITH

Arrogance. Pride is the emotion that occurs when I believe I've done something good and want to tell others. Arrogance is the emotion from which I want to tell others how much I know and that I am superior to them.

HOW IT FEELS OR MOVES US

To tell others about things we've done that we consider good

HOW OUR BODY MIGHT FEEL

Warm, energized, light, full

HOW OUR BREATH MIGHT BE

Full deep breaths, a little faster than resting rate

HOW OUR BODY MIGHT SHAPE ITSELF

Chin lifted up slightly, smiling, chest is full front and back, erect but relaxed

QUOTE

"Disciplining yourself to do what you know is right and important, although difficult, is the highroad to pride, self-esteem, and personal satisfaction."—Margaret Thatcher

PRUDENCE

ETYMOLOGICAL ROOT

From Latin *prudentia*, "a foreseeing, foresight, sagacity, practical judgment"

WHAT WE THINK OR SAY

"There might be danger, so best to move ahead cautiously."

ITS IMPACT ON OUR OPENNESS TO OTHERS

Neutral to closes us

OUR REACTION OR IMPULSE FOR ACTION IS…

To act cautiously

RELATED EMOTIONS

Modesty, timidity, anxiety

ITS PURPOSE IS TO…

Let us adjust to unknown situations or changing circumstances

THE TIME ORIENTATION OF THIS EMOTION IS…

Future

HOW THIS EMOTION CAN GET IN THE WAY

Prudence allows us to move ahead, paying close attention and at an appropriate velocity. It can also slow us down in situations where moving more quickly would produce more benefit.

EMOTIONS WE CONFUSE IT WITH

Modesty. Prudence means moving slowly to calculate the effect of action, whereas modesty is acting in a manner that avoids extremes.

HOW IT FEELS OR MOVES US

To move slowly, confirming at each step that the situation is safe

HOW OUR BODY MIGHT FEEL

Calm and alert

HOW OUR BREATH MIGHT BE

Shallow, slow

HOW OUR BODY MIGHT SHAPE ITSELF

Length diminished

QUOTE

"Do not trust all men, but trust men of worth; the former course is silly, the latter a mark of prudence."—Democritus

RAGE

The emotion is ....

ETYMOLOGICAL ROOT

From Latin *rabia*, "madness, fury"

WHAT WE THINK OR SAY

"Nothing is worth preserving."

ITS IMPACT ON OUR OPENNESS TO OTHERS

Closes us

OUR REACTION OR IMPULSE FOR ACTION IS...

To destroy

RELATED EMOTIONS

Fury, anger, hate

ITS PURPOSE IS TO...

Let us destroy

THE TIME ORIENTATION OF THIS EMOTION IS...

Present

HOW THIS EMOTION CAN GET IN THE WAY

Since rage is the belief that nothing is worth saving and thus should be destroyed, it ends all relationships and progress.

EMOTIONS WE CONFUSE IT WITH

Anger. Rage is the belief that "nothing is worth saving." Anger is the belief that "the person creating injustice should be punished."

HOW IT FEELS OR MOVES US

We can be literally blinded to what we are doing.

HOW OUR BODY MIGHT FEEL

Hot, flushed, tight jaw and chest and belly

HOW OUR BREATH MIGHT BE

Very fast, high in the chest

HOW OUR BODY MIGHT SHAPE ITSELF

Moving forward, fists clenched, length not grounded

QUOTE

"Their rage supplies them with weapons."—*Virgil*

REBELLIOUSNESS

ETYMOLOGICAL ROOT

From Latin *rebellis*, "insurgent, rebellious," from *rebellare*, "to rebel, revolt," from *re-* "opposite, against," + *bellare* "wage war"

WHAT WE THINK OR SAY

"I don't accept the rules."

ITS IMPACT ON OUR OPENNESS TO OTHERS

Closes us

OUR REACTION OR IMPULSE FOR ACTION IS...

To fight against rules and/or restrictions

RELATED EMOTIONS

Resentment, hate, mischievousness

ITS PURPOSE IS TO...

Let us break social convention

THE TIME ORIENTATION OF THIS EMOTION IS...

Present

HOW THIS EMOTION CAN GET IN THE WAY

Rebelliousness can be a balancing emotion and also helpful to right wrongs, although its way of doing so can create enemies and, in excess, becomes an end in itself.

EMOTIONS WE CONFUSE IT WITH

Cynicism. Rebelliousness is the emotion in which we "resist the system" no matter what that system is, whereas cynicism means that we doubt the good intentions of others and denigrate them.

HOW IT FEELS OR MOVES US

Restless, wanting to be free and not bound by others' standards

HOW OUR BODY MIGHT FEEL

Energized and focused

HOW OUR BREATH MIGHT BE

Fast-paced, deep breaths, open-mouthed

HOW OUR BODY MIGHT SHAPE ITSELF

Upward and forward direction, full length

QUOTE

"Literature is dangerous: it awakens a rebellious attitude in us."—Mario Vargas Llosa

REGRET

ETYMOLOGICAL ROOT

"To look back with distress or sorrowful longing; to grieve for on remembering," late 14c., from Old French *regreter*

WHAT WE THINK OR SAY

"If I had it to do over, I would do it differently."

ITS IMPACT ON OUR OPENNESS TO OTHERS

Closes us

OUR REACTION OR IMPULSE FOR ACTION IS...

To wish I'd done something differently

RELATED EMOTIONS

Remorse, wistfulness, nostalgia

ITS PURPOSE IS TO...

Let us reflect on the wisdom of past choices in order to make better ones in the future

THE TIME ORIENTATION OF THIS EMOTION IS...

Past

HOW THIS EMOTION CAN GET IN THE WAY

Regret tells us that we believe a different choice in the past would have been better than the one we made. If we listen to that message and use it as a guide, it can be helpful; otherwise it can produce constant pain, because we can never go back in time "to do what we should have done."

EMOTIONS WE CONFUSE IT WITH

Nostalgia. Regret means we believe that life would be better if we had/hadn't done a certain thing in the past. Nostalgia is the belief that life was better in the past and we'd like to go back in time.

HOW IT FEELS OR MOVES US

Without energy and self-blaming

HOW OUR BODY MIGHT FEEL

Tired, heavy, slow

HOW OUR BREATH MIGHT BE

Mid-chest, slow, even

HOW OUR BODY MIGHT SHAPE ITSELF

Head down, shoulders stooped, concave chest

QUOTE

"I'd rather regret the things I've done than regret the things I haven't done."—Lucille Ball

REMORSE

ETYMOLOGICAL ROOT

From Latin *remordere* "to vex, disturb," literally "to bite back,"
from *re-* "back" + *mordere* "to bite"

WHAT WE THINK OR SAY

"I shouldn't have done that."

ITS IMPACT ON OUR OPENNESS TO OTHERS

Closes us

OUR REACTION OR IMPULSE FOR ACTION IS...

To blame myself for past actions
or things I've said

RELATED EMOTIONS

Regret, wistfulness, nostalgia

ITS PURPOSE IS TO...

Show us which past behaviors we
would change if we could

THE TIME ORIENTATION OF THIS EMOTION IS...

Past

HOW THIS EMOTION CAN GET IN THE WAY

Remorse is much like regret but is also related to guilt. It can become the source of self-punishment rather than a guide to how we would like to live.

EMOTIONS WE CONFUSE IT WITH

Regret. Remorse literally means "to bite back," as when we wish we could take back words we have spoken. Regret means we believe the present would be better if we had or hadn't done something in the past.

HOW IT FEELS OR MOVES US

To punish ourselves for choices we made in the past

HOW OUR BODY MIGHT FEEL

Tired, heavy, slow

HOW OUR BREATH MIGHT BE

Mid-chest, slow, even

HOW OUR BODY MIGHT SHAPE ITSELF

Concave chest, shoulders hunched, head down

QUOTE

"There is no person so severely punished, as those who subject themselves to the whip of their own remorse."
—*Lucius Annaeus Seneca*

RESENTMENT

ETYMOLOGICAL ROOT

From Latin *re-+ sentire* "to feel"

WHAT WE THINK OR SAY

"It shouldn't be like this; this is unfair; I shouldn't have to do this."

ITS IMPACT ON OUR OPENNESS TO OTHERS

Closes us

OUR REACTION OR IMPULSE FOR ACTION IS...

To resist and get even

RELATED EMOTIONS

Anger, vengeance, hate

ITS PURPOSE IS TO...

Identify what we believe is fair and unfair

THE TIME ORIENTATION OF THIS EMOTION IS...

Past

HOW THIS EMOTION CAN GET IN THE WAY

The impulse of resentment is "to get even." It is based on the belief that something was unfair. It can happen that we damage relationships getting even for something that didn't occur as we thought.

EMOTIONS WE CONFUSE IT WITH

Anger. Resentment is concerned with perceived unfairness, while anger is concerned with perceived injustice.

HOW IT FEELS OR MOVES US

We take actions we believe will help us "get even" for the unfairness we've experienced.

HOW OUR BODY MIGHT FEEL

Tight shoulders, jaw, belly

HOW OUR BREATH MIGHT BE

Slow, even, belly breath

HOW OUR BODY MIGHT SHAPE ITSELF

Leaning forward, eyes narrowed and focused, concave chest, length is shortened

QUOTE

"Resentment is like drinking poison and waiting for the other person to die."—Saint Augustine

RESIGNATION

ETYMOLOGICAL ROOT

From Latin *resignare*, "to check off, annul, cancel, give back, give up," from *re-* "opposite" + *signare* "to make an entry in an account book," literally "to mark"

WHAT WE THINK OR SAY

"Nothing I do will make any difference, so why try?"

ITS IMPACT ON OUR OPENNESS TO OTHERS

Closes us

OUR REACTION OR IMPULSE FOR ACTION IS…

To give up

RELATED EMOTIONS

Despair, cynicism, hopelessness

ITS PURPOSE IS TO…

Allow us to surrender and save our energy

THE TIME ORIENTATION OF THIS EMOTION IS…

Past

HOW THIS EMOTION CAN GET IN THE WAY

Resignation does not mean there are not possibilities, but only that I cannot see the possibilities. In resignation we give up and do not act because it seems pointless.

EMOTIONS WE CONFUSE IT WITH

Apathy. Apathy is the emotion in which we don't care or aren't aware of our passion. Resignation is the belief that nothing we do will make a difference.

HOW IT FEELS OR MOVES US

We throw up our hands and quit trying.

HOW OUR BODY MIGHT FEEL

Heavy, slow, direction of back and down

HOW OUR BREATH MIGHT BE

Slow, shallow, sighing

HOW OUR BODY MIGHT SHAPE ITSELF

Length is very diminished, shoulders hunched, concave chest

QUOTE

"I can imagine no more comfortable frame of mind for the conduct of life than a humorous resignation."
—W. Somerset Maugham

RESPECT

ETYMOLOGICAL ROOT

From Latin *respectus*, "regard, a looking at," literally "act of looking back (or often) at one"

WHAT WE THINK OR SAY

"This thing or person deserves to be treated as important."

ITS IMPACT ON OUR OPENNESS TO OTHERS

Opens us

OUR REACTION OR IMPULSE FOR ACTION IS...

To treat with honor or high regard

RELATED EMOTIONS

Dignity, reverence, love

ITS PURPOSE IS TO...

Allow us to legitimize others

THE TIME ORIENTATION OF THIS EMOTION IS...

Past or present

HOW THIS EMOTION CAN GET IN THE WAY

If our standard for respect is low, it will mean that we extend respect to many or all. We may also have a low level of respect for ourselves, which could mean we allow others to treat us poorly.

EMOTIONS WE CONFUSE IT WITH

Admiration. Respect means we hold a positive image of someone for their past behavior. We believe they are worthy. Admiration means we look up to them and would like to be as they are or do as they do.

HOW IT FEELS OR MOVES US

We listen well in an effort to understand and treat others as worthy.

HOW OUR BODY MIGHT FEEL

Relaxed, alert, calm

HOW OUR BREATH MIGHT BE

Even, steady breathing

HOW OUR BODY MIGHT SHAPE ITSELF

Open, head up, chest full, length full, depth full

QUOTE

"One of the most sincere forms of respect is actually listening to what another has to say."—Bryant H. McGill

REVERENCE

The emotion is....

ETYMOLOGICAL ROOT

From Latin *revereri*, "to stand in awe of, respect, honor, fear, be afraid of"

WHAT WE THINK OR SAY

"This is worthy of my respect."

ITS IMPACT ON OUR OPENNESS TO OTHERS

Opens us

OUR REACTION OR IMPULSE FOR ACTION IS...

To treat with respect

RELATED EMOTIONS

Admiration, love, adoration

ITS PURPOSE IS TO...

Tell us what we believe is worthy of our respect and honor

THE TIME ORIENTATION OF THIS EMOTION IS...

Present

HOW THIS EMOTION CAN GET IN THE WAY

Reverence can blind us to our own needs. Our attention is singularly focused on a being or institution rather than being balanced with a focus on ourselves.

EMOTIONS WE CONFUSE IT WITH

Adoration. Adoration means we worship another as superior, whereas reverence means we consider them deserving of respect.

HOW IT FEELS OR MOVES US

We are quiet, listening and attentive to the value of the other.

HOW OUR BODY MIGHT FEEL

Calm, energized

HOW OUR BREATH MIGHT BE

Slow, even, belly breath

HOW OUR BODY MIGHT SHAPE ITSELF

Open chest and arms, perhaps lowered head, but otherwise full length and width and depth

QUOTE

"Let parents bequeath to their children not riches, but the spirit of reverence."—Plato

REVULSION

ETYMOLOGICAL ROOT

From Latin *revulsionem*, "a tearing off, act of pulling away"

WHAT WE THINK OR SAY

"I can't look."

ITS IMPACT ON OUR OPENNESS TO OTHERS

Closes us

OUR REACTION OR IMPULSE FOR ACTION IS...

To turn away from

RELATED EMOTIONS

Disgust, distaste, hate

ITS PURPOSE IS TO...

Tell us what is too awful to see

THE TIME ORIENTATION OF THIS EMOTION IS...

Present

HOW THIS EMOTION CAN GET IN THE WAY

In revulsion we are unable to remain in the presence of the person or situation. It would not be a helpful emotion for someone needing to be at the scene of disasters or civic emergencies.

EMOTIONS WE CONFUSE IT WITH

Hate. Revulsion is the emotion that makes us unable to look at a thing, while hate is the emotion that has us avoiding it altogether.

HOW IT FEELS OR MOVES US

Unable to look or engage

HOW OUR BODY MIGHT FEEL

To move away, to feel queasy

HOW OUR BREATH MIGHT BE

Very shallow or possibly stopped

HOW OUR BODY MIGHT SHAPE ITSELF

Width is diminished, head down, length is shortened

QUOTE

"The marker of our time is its revulsion against imposed patterns."—Marshall McLuhan

RIGHTEOUSNESS

ETYMOLOGICAL ROOT

Early 16c. alteration of *rightwise*, from Old English *rihtwis*, from *riht* + *wis* "wise, way, manner"

WHAT WE THINK OR SAY

"There is one morally correct way."

ITS IMPACT ON OUR OPENNESS TO OTHERS

Closes us

OUR REACTION OR IMPULSE FOR ACTION IS…

To act according to what we believe is morally correct

RELATED EMOTIONS

Arrogance, certainty

ITS PURPOSE IS TO…

Let us be sure of our beliefs

THE TIME ORIENTATION OF THIS EMOTION IS…

Present

HOW THIS EMOTION CAN GET IN THE WAY

The implication of "I believe I am right" is that everyone else is wrong. That is the danger of righteousness. Although it is attractive to some people because of its certainty, it alienates others.

EMOTIONS WE CONFUSE IT WITH

Arrogance. Righteousness means I believe I know "the Truth," which means others need to do what I say is right. Arrogance means I believe I know more or am smarter and so should be considered a superior being.

HOW IT FEELS OR MOVES US

To act as if we know the universal truth

HOW OUR BODY MIGHT FEEL

Upright, expanded depth, length extended and grounded

HOW OUR BREATH MIGHT BE

Breath is high in the chest, medium/fast-paced

HOW OUR BODY MIGHT SHAPE ITSELF

Upright, rigid, closed

QUOTE

"What is important is man should live in righteousness, in natural love for mankind."—Bob Marley

SADNESS

ETYMOLOGICAL ROOT

From Old English *sæd*, "sated, full, having had one's fill (of food, drink, fighting, etc.), weary of"

WHAT WE THINK OR SAY

"I've lost something I care about."

ITS IMPACT ON OUR OPENNESS TO OTHERS

Closes us

OUR REACTION OR IMPULSE FOR ACTION IS...

To grieve

RELATED EMOTIONS

Melancholy, despair, anguish

ITS PURPOSE IS TO...

Show us what is important to us

THE TIME ORIENTATION OF THIS EMOTION IS...

Past

HOW THIS EMOTION CAN GET IN THE WAY

The impulse of sadness is to remove ourselves from action and grieve. This allows us to come to terms with our loss, but if it becomes a mood, it will cut us off from others.

EMOTIONS WE CONFUSE IT WITH

Despair. Sadness means we've lost something we care about. Despair means we've lost hope that things will improve.

HOW IT FEELS OR MOVES US

Low energy with a desire to be alone

HOW OUR BODY MIGHT FEEL

Downward direction

HOW OUR BREATH MIGHT BE

Short, quick, shallow breaths in succession

HOW OUR BODY MIGHT SHAPE ITSELF

Shoulders slumped, width and length diminished, chest concave

QUOTE

"Sadness is but a wall between two gardens."—Khalil Gibran

SATISFACTION

The emotion i.

WHAT WE THINK OR SAY

"I have enough."

ITS IMPACT ON OUR OPENNESS TO OTHERS

Opens us

OUR REACTION OR IMPULSE FOR ACTION IS...

To savor

RELATED EMOTIONS

Contentment, acceptance, pride

ITS PURPOSE IS TO...

Inform us when we have enough

THE TIME ORIENTATION OF THIS EMOTION IS...

Present

HOW THIS EMOTION CAN GET IN THE WAY

Feeling satisfaction can be a signal to stop whatever activity we are in—eating, working, exercising—and it can lead to mediocrity or complacency.

EMOTIONS WE CONFUSE IT WITH

Happiness. Satisfaction means we believe we "have enough," whereas happiness means we like how life is turning out.

HOW IT FEELS OR MOVES US

To feel calm and move on to other projects

HOW OUR BODY MIGHT FEEL

Relaxed, warm, maybe flush

HOW OUR BREATH MIGHT BE

Slow, easy breathing

HOW OUR BODY MIGHT SHAPE ITSELF

Length, width, and depth are balanced. Open, head erect, eyes forward

QUOTE

"It is surprising to notice that even from the earliest age, man finds the greatest satisfaction in feeling independent."
—*Maria Montessori*

SCORN

ETYMOLOGICAL ROOT

"To break off (someone's) horns," from Vulgar Latin *excornare*, *ex-* "without" + *cornu* "horn"

WHAT WE THINK OR SAY

"This person is not worthy of my respect."

ITS IMPACT ON OUR OPENNESS TO OTHERS

Closes us

OUR REACTION OR IMPULSE FOR ACTION IS...

To insult

RELATED EMOTIONS

Contempt, hate, disdain

ITS PURPOSE IS TO...

Tell us we believe someone is not worthy of respect

THE TIME ORIENTATION OF THIS EMOTION IS...

Past or present

HOW THIS EMOTION CAN GET IN THE WAY

To diminish others (or oneself) with scorn makes an unguarded relationship difficult or impossible.

EMOTIONS WE CONFUSE IT WITH

Contempt. Scorn comes from the root "to remove one's horns" or insult someone, whereas contempt means to despise and disrespect.

HOW IT FEELS OR MOVES US

We tend to look down on or condescend to the other.

HOW OUR BODY MIGHT FEEL

Tight and closed in the chest

HOW OUR BREATH MIGHT BE

Rapid, shallow breathing

HOW OUR BODY MIGHT SHAPE ITSELF

Eyes narrowed, brow furrowed

QUOTE

"Silence is the most perfect expression of scorn."
—*George Bernard Shaw*

SENTIMENTALITY

ETYMOLOGICAL ROOT

From Medieval Latin *sentimentum*, "feeling, affection, opinion," from Latin *sentire*, "to feel"

WHAT WE THINK OR SAY

"I feel tender when I think about this."

ITS IMPACT ON OUR OPENNESS TO OTHERS

Opens us

OUR REACTION OR IMPULSE FOR ACTION IS...

To think about tenderly

RELATED EMOTIONS

Nostalgia, wistfulness, tenderness

ITS PURPOSE IS TO...

Show what we feel tender about

THE TIME ORIENTATION OF THIS EMOTION IS...

Past

HOW THIS EMOTION CAN GET IN THE WAY

Sentimentality means that we have an attachment or feelings to something or someone. In a sense, it interferes with our ability to understand things based on logic.

EMOTIONS WE CONFUSE IT WITH

Nostalgia. Sentimental means "to have feelings of affection," whereas nostalgia means we believe the past was better than the present and wish we could return there.

HOW IT FEELS OR MOVES US

Quiet and handling with care

HOW OUR BODY MIGHT FEEL

Downward and towards movement, length somewhat diminished, heart and chest open

HOW OUR BREATH MIGHT BE

Slow, relaxed belly breathing

HOW OUR BODY MIGHT SHAPE ITSELF

Open chest, full depth

QUOTE

"If you think my music is sentimental and self-absorbed, I agree with you."—James Taylor

SERENITY

ETYMOLOGICAL ROOT

From Latin *serenus*, "peaceful, calm, clear"

WHAT WE THINK OR SAY

"I feel such peace."

ITS IMPACT ON OUR OPENNESS TO OTHERS

Neutral

OUR REACTION OR IMPULSE FOR ACTION IS...

To rest and relax

RELATED EMOTIONS

Calmness, peace, acceptance

ITS PURPOSE IS TO...

Let us rest in peace

THE TIME ORIENTATION OF THIS EMOTION IS...

Present

HOW THIS EMOTION CAN GET IN THE WAY

In serenity, calmness, and peace we can be unaware of tensions or dangers around us. In these emotions they disappear or are not part of our experience.

EMOTIONS WE CONFUSE IT WITH

Acceptance. Acceptance means we believe that "things are as they are," although we may not like it or agree with it. Serenity is an emotion in which we feel calm, clear, and without care.

HOW IT FEELS OR MOVES US

Quiet, calm, unworried

HOW OUR BODY MIGHT FEEL

Complete relaxation, with full awareness, calm

HOW OUR BREATH MIGHT BE

Even, slow, full

HOW OUR BODY MIGHT SHAPE ITSELF

Very open arms and chest and face, smile, gaze is far off

QUOTE

"Every breath we take, every step we make, can be filled with peace, joy and serenity."—Thich Nhat Hanh

SHAME

ETYMOLOGICAL ROOT

The best guess is that this is from PIE *skem-*, from *kem-* "to cover" (covering oneself being a common expression of shame).

WHAT WE THINK OR SAY

"I broke the standards of my community."

ITS IMPACT ON OUR OPENNESS TO OTHERS

Closes us

OUR REACTION OR IMPULSE FOR ACTION IS...

To hide from the judgment and/or punishment I expect from others

RELATED EMOTIONS

Guilt, embarrassment, mortification

ITS PURPOSE IS TO...

Tell me when I've broken a norm or standard of the community

THE TIME ORIENTATION OF THIS EMOTION IS...

Past or present

HOW THIS EMOTION CAN GET IN THE WAY

Shame, in this interpretation, isn't about what is morally correct or incorrect. It occurs when we break a rule of the community we are a part of. It feels as if "we are wrong" but needs to be put into this context to assess dispassionately.

EMOTIONS WE CONFUSE IT WITH

Guilt. These two are often reversed, but guilt means I have acted in a way that is not aligned with my personal values, whereas shame means I've acted in a way that is out of alignment with the values of a community I belong to.

HOW IT FEELS OR MOVES US

Flushed face, red cheeks, sensation of heat, fearing punishment of the community

HOW OUR BODY MIGHT FEEL

Flushed, heavy

HOW OUR BREATH MIGHT BE

Shallow, weak

HOW OUR BODY MIGHT SHAPE ITSELF

Head hung down, shoulders slumped, chest caved in

QUOTE

"Being ignorant is not so much a shame as being unwilling to learn."—Benjamin Franklin

291

SHYNESS

ETYMOLOGICAL ROOT

Late Old English *sceoh*, "timid, easily startled," German *scheuchen*, "to scare away"

WHAT WE THINK OR SAY

"I don't want others to see me."

ITS IMPACT ON OUR OPENNESS TO OTHERS

Closes us

OUR REACTION OR IMPULSE FOR ACTION IS...

To hide

RELATED EMOTIONS

Prudence, caution, embarrassment

ITS PURPOSE IS TO...

Remain safe when being seen might be dangerous

THE TIME ORIENTATION OF THIS EMOTION IS...

Present

HOW THIS EMOTION CAN GET IN THE WAY

Shyness can keep us "in the corner and out of sight" and thus deprive us of interactions and possibilities. This is well known by others, but the shy person may be unaware of their potential loss.

EMOTIONS WE CONFUSE IT WITH

Timidity. In shyness we simply don't like to be seen because it makes us uncomfortable. Timidity is the desire to remain hidden because of fear.

HOW IT FEELS OR MOVES US

To remain out of sight as much as possible

HOW OUR BODY MIGHT FEEL

Warm and flush

HOW OUR BREATH MIGHT BE

High and shallow, and tight

HOW OUR BODY MIGHT SHAPE ITSELF

Turning away and in, chest covered, head lowered, eyes cast down and peeking to see if the other person has noticed you

QUOTE

"Shyness is invariably a suppression of something. It's almost a fear of what you're capable of."—Rhys Ifans

SKEPTICISM

The emotion is.......

WHAT WE THINK OR SAY

"I'm don't know whether I should believe this or not."

ITS IMPACT ON OUR OPENNESS TO OTHERS

Closes us

OUR REACTION OR IMPULSE FOR ACTION IS…

To question the validity of a point of view

RELATED EMOTIONS

Cynicism, rebelliousness, resentment

ITS PURPOSE IS TO…

Help us distinguish what to believe

THE TIME ORIENTATION OF THIS EMOTION IS…

Present

HOW THIS EMOTION CAN GET IN THE WAY

There are two main ways of coming to an understanding. One is through curiosity and the other is through skepticism. The danger of skepticism is that it is often seen as a "negative" emotion, and people do not see it as contributing to moving forward.

EMOTIONS WE CONFUSE IT WITH

Cynicism. Skepticism occurs when we are faced with a choice between a belief we hold and a new option. Cynicism is an inability to believe others' good intentions and the desire to recruit others to our view.

HOW IT FEELS OR MOVES US

To question or hesitate to believe something new

HOW OUR BODY MIGHT FEEL

Tightness in the jaw and shoulders and neck, width contracted

HOW OUR BREATH MIGHT BE

Shallow, moderate pace

HOW OUR BODY MIGHT SHAPE ITSELF

Concave chest, head tilted to one side, eyes focused

QUOTE

"She believed in nothing; only her skepticism kept her from being an atheist."—Jean-Paul Sartre

STUBBORNNESS

ETYMOLOGICAL ROOT

Possibly from Old English *stybb*, "stump of a tree"

WHAT WE THINK OR SAY

"I'm going to remain as I am, believing what I do."

ITS IMPACT ON OUR OPENNESS TO OTHERS

Closes us

OUR REACTION OR IMPULSE FOR ACTION IS…

To insist

RELATED EMOTIONS

Certainty, rectitude, righteousness

ITS PURPOSE IS TO…

Let us be inflexible

THE TIME ORIENTATION OF THIS EMOTION IS…

Present, future

HOW THIS EMOTION CAN GET IN THE WAY

Unwillingness to change can be a benefit allowing us to stand our ground when we believe deeply, but it can also alienate others or close possibilities that we might benefit from.

EMOTIONS WE CONFUSE IT WITH

Righteousness. Stubbornness is the unwillingness to change our belief or actions, whereas righteousness is the belief that we know the morally correct way to behave and others should do as we say.

HOW IT FEELS OR MOVES US

To stay as we are

HOW OUR BODY MIGHT FEEL

Tight jaw and back, energy in the feet

HOW OUR BREATH MIGHT BE

Fast, even, mid-chest

HOW OUR BODY MIGHT SHAPE ITSELF

Shoulders raised, length shortened, width contracted

QUOTE

"I have yet to meet anyone quite so stubborn as myself and animated by this overpowering passion that leaves me no time for thought or anything else. I have, in fact, no interest in life outside racing cars."—Enzo Ferrari

SURPRISE

ETYMOLOGICAL ROOT

From *sur-* "over" + *prendre* "to take," from Latin *prendere*,
contracted from *prehendere* "to grasp, seize"

WHAT WE THINK OR SAY

"I didn't expect that!"

ITS IMPACT ON OUR OPENNESS TO OTHERS

Opens us

OUR REACTION OR IMPULSE FOR ACTION IS...

To momentarily disbelieve

RELATED EMOTIONS

Delight, happiness, incredulity

ITS PURPOSE IS TO...

Inform us when something
unexpected has happened

THE TIME ORIENTATION OF THIS EMOTION IS...

Present

HOW THIS EMOTION CAN GET IN THE WAY

Surprise can throw us off balance emotionally, mentally, or physically. A big shock can take some time to recover from, and some create a change in our being. This can occur from surprises we assess as positive or negative.

EMOTIONS WE CONFUSE IT WITH

Disappointment. Disappointment occurs when something we want to happen doesn't occur, whereas surprise is the occurrence of something we didn't expect or imagine and could be positive or negative.

HOW IT FEELS OR MOVES US

We may jump or react in a startled way.

HOW OUR BODY MIGHT FEEL

Energy high in the chest and head, light in the feet

HOW OUR BREATH MIGHT BE

Fast, shallow intake

HOW OUR BODY MIGHT SHAPE ITSELF

Move back and away

QUOTE

"Surprise is the greatest gift which life can grant us."
—Boris Pasternak

SYMPATHY

ETYMOLOGICAL ROOT

From Greek *sympatheia*, "fellow-feeling, community of feeling," from *sympathes* "affected by like feelings," from assimilated form of *syn-* "together" + *pathos* "feeling"

WHAT WE THINK OR SAY

"I have experienced something similar."

ITS IMPACT ON OUR OPENNESS TO OTHERS

Opens us

OUR REACTION OR IMPULSE FOR ACTION IS...

To acknowledge others' emotions

RELATED EMOTIONS

Care, compassion, empathy

ITS PURPOSE IS TO...

Let us identify with the emotions of another

THE TIME ORIENTATION OF THIS EMOTION IS...

Present

HOW THIS EMOTION CAN GET IN THE WAY

Sympathy can get in the way if the emotion that is needed is compassion. In sympathy we resonate with the other person and can understand their situation, because it is similar to something we have experienced.

EMOTIONS WE CONFUSE IT WITH

Empathy. Empathy allows us to "feel what the other is feeling" and sympathy allows us to "understand what the other is feeling."

HOW IT FEELS OR MOVES US

We offer understanding.

HOW OUR BODY MIGHT FEEL

Relaxed, alert, calm

HOW OUR BREATH MIGHT BE

Even, slow, belly breath

HOW OUR BODY MIGHT SHAPE ITSELF

Open arms and chest, full length and depth

QUOTE

"A sympathetic friend can be quite as dear as a brother."
—Homer

TENDERNESS

ETYMOLOGICAL ROOT

From Latin *tenerem*, "soft, delicate; of tender age, youthful"

WHAT WE THINK OR SAY

"You are safe." "It will be all right."

ITS IMPACT ON OUR OPENNESS TO OTHERS

Opens us

OUR REACTION OR IMPULSE FOR ACTION IS...

To provide safety for others

RELATED EMOTIONS

Kindness, adoration, love

ITS PURPOSE IS TO...

Allow us to provide a sense of safety to others

THE TIME ORIENTATION OF THIS EMOTION IS...

Present

HOW THIS EMOTION CAN GET IN THE WAY

Tenderness is the emotion that prompts us to create safety for others. At times this can be misinterpreted (by us or by them) as affection or even passion, and it can produce undesirable consequences.

EMOTIONS WE CONFUSE IT WITH

Kindness. Tenderness is the emotion in which we create safety for others physically or emotionally. Kindness is welcoming or treating others as if they are our relatives or we have feelings of closeness for them.

HOW IT FEELS OR MOVES US

To embrace and protect others

HOW OUR BODY MIGHT FEEL

Soft, open

HOW OUR BREATH MIGHT BE

Slow, even pace

HOW OUR BODY MIGHT SHAPE ITSELF

Leaning in, warm

QUOTE

"There is no charm equal to tenderness of heart."
—*Jane Austen*

TERROR

ETYMOLOGICAL ROOT

From Latin *terrorem*, "great fear, dread, alarm, panic; object of fear, cause of alarm; terrible news," from *terrere*, "fill with fear, frighten"

WHAT WE THINK OR SAY

"I'm certain something horrible is going to happen."

ITS IMPACT ON OUR OPENNESS TO OTHERS

Closes us

OUR REACTION OR IMPULSE FOR ACTION IS...

To avoid or run away

RELATED EMOTIONS

Dread, fear, horror

ITS PURPOSE IS TO...

Let us avoid immediate threats

THE TIME ORIENTATION OF THIS EMOTION IS...

Future

HOW THIS EMOTION CAN GET IN THE WAY

Terror can keep us away from situations that could prove dangerous, but it can also restrict our movements and leave us isolated.

EMOTIONS WE CONFUSE IT WITH

Dread. Terror is the anticipation of an event that we believe will harm us. Dread is anxiety about what may happen if we proceed.

HOW IT FEELS OR MOVES US

Move away quickly or freeze

HOW OUR BODY MIGHT FEEL

Tight in the gut and chest

HOW OUR BREATH MIGHT BE

High and fast

HOW OUR BODY MIGHT SHAPE ITSELF

Eyes and mouth wide open, arms protecting the head

QUOTE

"The risk of wrong decision is preferable to the terror of indecision."—Maimonides

THANKFULNESS

ETYMOLOGICAL ROOT

Old English *pancian*, *poncian*, "to give thanks, to recompense, reward"

WHAT WE THINK OR SAY

"I appreciate what you did for me."

ITS IMPACT ON OUR OPENNESS TO OTHERS

Opens us

- - - - - - - - - - - - - - - - - - -   -

OUR REACTION OR IMPULSE FOR ACTION IS...

To engage in mutual exchange

RELATED EMOTIONS

Gratitude, appreciation

- - - - - - - - - - - - - - - - - - -   -

ITS PURPOSE IS TO...

Acknowledge an exchange of like value

THE TIME ORIENTATION OF THIS EMOTION IS...

Past

- -

HOW THIS EMOTION CAN GET IN THE WAY

Overuse of thanks can diminish the power of it as an emotion and make it impotent when it is needed.

EMOTIONS WE CONFUSE IT WITH

Appreciation. Thankfulness prompts us to express our appreciation for a trade of equal value. Appreciation is the belief that something is of value.

HOW IT FEELS OR MOVES US

To show appreciation

HOW OUR BODY MIGHT FEEL

Relaxed alert, energized, warm

HOW OUR BREATH MIGHT BE

Deep, slow, even breathing

HOW OUR BODY MIGHT SHAPE ITSELF

Open chest, arms, face, eyes; length, width and depth all balanced

QUOTE

"All our discontents about what we want appeared to spring from the want of thankfulness for what we have."
—*Daniel Defoe*

TIMIDITY

The emotion is.............

WHAT WE THINK OR SAY

"I'll be safer if I'm hidden."

ITS IMPACT ON OUR OPENNESS TO OTHERS

Closes us

OUR REACTION OR IMPULSE FOR ACTION IS...

To hide or stay on the periphery

RELATED EMOTIONS

Shyness, embarrassment, anxiety, fear

ITS PURPOSE IS TO...

Let us observe from a distance to gauge level of danger

THE TIME ORIENTATION OF THIS EMOTION IS...

Present

HOW THIS EMOTION CAN GET IN THE WAY

Timidity keeps us safe—or at least that is what we think when we feel timid—but it doesn't allow us to be seen or to develop relationships and make offers.

EMOTIONS WE CONFUSE IT WITH

Anxiety. Timidity is the belief that we are safer unseen, and anxiety is the belief that something may harm us, although we can't identify what.

HOW IT FEELS OR MOVES US

Hesitate to engage until we are sure it is safe

HOW OUR BODY MIGHT FEEL

Shrinking from

HOW OUR BREATH MIGHT BE

Shallow, short, medium-paced

HOW OUR BODY MIGHT SHAPE ITSELF

Length and width diminished

QUOTE

"The first symptom of love in a young man is timidity; in a girl boldness."—*Victor Hugo*

TOLERANCE

ETYMOLOGICAL ROOT

From Latin *tolerare*, "to endure, sustain, support, suffer," literally "to bear"

WHAT WE THINK OR SAY

"I'll put up with it until it changes."

ITS IMPACT ON OUR OPENNESS TO OTHERS

Opens us

OUR REACTION OR IMPULSE FOR ACTION IS...

To put up with

RELATED EMOTIONS

Acceptance, patience, calmness

ITS PURPOSE IS TO...

Allow us to put up with things we don't enjoy or agree with

THE TIME ORIENTATION OF THIS EMOTION IS...

Present

HOW THIS EMOTION CAN GET IN THE WAY

Putting up with something is useful as long as the "something" isn't damaging in the long term. If it is, then shifting to an emotion such as anger, resentment, or ambition may be helpful.

EMOTIONS WE CONFUSE IT WITH

Acceptance. Tolerance is the willingness "to put up with a situation until it changes," whereas acceptance is to declare "it is as it is," even if we don't like it or agree with it.

HOW IT FEELS OR MOVES US

To endure things we find unpleasant

HOW OUR BODY MIGHT FEEL

Relaxed but alert

HOW OUR BREATH MIGHT BE

Even, slow, belly breath

HOW OUR BODY MIGHT SHAPE ITSELF

Width somewhat contracted

QUOTE

"In the practice of tolerance, one's enemy is the best teacher."—Dalai Lama

TRUST

ETYMOLOGICAL ROOT

From Old Norse *traust*, "help, confidence, protection, support," and Old High German *trost*, "fidelity"

WHAT WE THINK OR SAY

"I'm not taking excessive risk."

ITS IMPACT ON OUR OPENNESS TO OTHERS

Opens us

OUR REACTION OR IMPULSE FOR ACTION IS...

To coordinate action or interact

RELATED EMOTIONS

Confidence, certainty, serenity

ITS PURPOSE IS TO...

Let us interact with others

THE TIME ORIENTATION OF THIS EMOTION IS...

Present

HOW THIS EMOTION CAN GET IN THE WAY

More trust is not always better. Too much trust exposes you to excessive risk. Not enough trust makes us blind to opportunities and closes off possibilities.

EMOTIONS WE CONFUSE IT WITH

Loyalty. Trust is the assessment that we are not taking undue risk or acting imprudently. Loyalty is the willingness to defend the boundaries of a community of which we are a part.

HOW IT FEELS OR MOVES US

We move ahead with confidence and sureness.

HOW OUR BODY MIGHT FEEL

Open and energized

HOW OUR BREATH MIGHT BE

Slow, even and steady

HOW OUR BODY MIGHT SHAPE ITSELF

Open chest area front and back of body. Full length and depth

QUOTE

"The best way to find out if you can trust somebody is to trust them."—Ernest Hemingway

UNCERTAINTY

ETYMOLOGICAL ROOT

From Vulgar Latin *certanus*, from Latin *certus*, "sure, fixed, settled, determined" + *un* "not"

WHAT WE THINK OR SAY

"I'm not sure which option will be the better one."

ITS IMPACT ON OUR OPENNESS TO OTHERS

Neutral

OUR REACTION OR IMPULSE FOR ACTION IS...

To hesitate

RELATED EMOTIONS

Doubt, anxiety, pessimism

ITS PURPOSE IS TO...

Tell us when the path to take is unclear

THE TIME ORIENTATION OF THIS EMOTION IS...

Future

HOW THIS EMOTION CAN GET IN THE WAY

Uncertainty can become a habit. When we practice uncertainty, we come to be uncertain. When we live in uncertainty, we are unable to take a stand for what we believe in and are unable to cultivate the emotion of dignity.

EMOTIONS WE CONFUSE IT WITH

Doubt. Doubt means we "are not sure because we are in a new territory," but it passes as we come to know the domain. Uncertainty is an unsureness about which choice would be better for us to take and may not depend on our knowledge of the domain.

HOW IT FEELS OR MOVES US

We hesitate and sometimes feel stuck or off balance.

HOW OUR BODY MIGHT FEEL

Tight

HOW OUR BREATH MIGHT BE

Medium depth to the breath, slow-paced

HOW OUR BODY MIGHT SHAPE ITSELF

Length and width diminished

QUOTE

"Exploring the unknown requires tolerating uncertainty."
—Brian Greene

URGENCY

ETYMOLOGICAL ROOT

From Latin *urgentem*, "to press hard"

WHAT WE THINK OR SAY

"It needs to be done now!"

ITS IMPACT ON OUR OPENNESS TO OTHERS

Closes us

OUR REACTION OR IMPULSE FOR ACTION IS...

Move very rapidly

RELATED EMOTIONS

Panic, terror, fear

ITS PURPOSE IS TO...

Take care of emergencies

THE TIME ORIENTATION OF THIS EMOTION IS...

Present

HOW THIS EMOTION CAN GET IN THE WAY

Urgency, if a habit, can cause us to act with unnecessary velocity, waste energy, and miss important clues. Urgency is an emotion that focuses on the outcome and sometimes overlooks the impact on the people involved.

EMOTIONS WE CONFUSE IT WITH

Panic. Urgency means "to press hard," which prompts us to move toward an objective with as much speed as possible. Panic prompts us to move quickly but does not give us direction or purpose except survival.

HOW IT FEELS OR MOVES US

Act rapidly

HOW OUR BODY MIGHT FEEL

Greatly energized

HOW OUR BREATH MIGHT BE

Fast-paced, high in the chest

HOW OUR BODY MIGHT SHAPE ITSELF

Moving forward, full length, width, and depth

QUOTE

"Life's most persistent and urgent question is, 'What are you doing for others?'"—Martin Luther King, Jr.

VENGEANCE

ETYMOLOGICAL ROOT

From Latin *vindicare*, "vindicate" from *vim dicare* "to show authority," from *vim*, accusative of *vis* "force" + root of *dicere* "to say"

WHAT WE THINK OR SAY

"I will get even for this."

ITS IMPACT ON OUR OPENNESS TO OTHERS

Closes us

OUR REACTION OR IMPULSE FOR ACTION IS...

To punish as a way to get even

RELATED EMOTIONS

Resentment, jealousy, hate

ITS PURPOSE IS TO...

Allow us to get even with others

THE TIME ORIENTATION OF THIS EMOTION IS...

Future

HOW THIS EMOTION CAN GET IN THE WAY

Saint Augustine is quoted as saying that "revenge is like taking poison and waiting for the other person to die." The caustic nature of revenge can drain our energy and cause us more suffering than the person we would like to punish.

EMOTIONS WE CONFUSE IT WITH

Resentment. Vengeance means we believe we have the right to get even for past events by punishing the source. Resentment means we believe something is unfair and getting even is a way of correcting the unfairness.

HOW IT FEELS OR MOVES US

To look for ways to hurt or punish another person

HOW OUR BODY MIGHT FEEL

Tight in the neck, shoulders, and gut

HOW OUR BREATH MIGHT BE

High in the chest, short and fast

HOW OUR BODY MIGHT SHAPE ITSELF

Moving towards, full length, and depth, width is exaggerated

QUOTE

"Control thy passions lest they take vengeance on thee."
—*Epictetus*

WISTFULNESS

ETYMOLOGICAL ROOT

Middle English *wistful* meant "bountiful, well-supplied," from Old English *wist*, "provisions"

WHAT WE THINK OR SAY

"I remember past times with tenderness and longing."

ITS IMPACT ON OUR OPENNESS TO OTHERS

Opens us

OUR REACTION OR IMPULSE FOR ACTION IS...

To long for something/someone we don't have any longer

RELATED EMOTIONS

Nostalgia, regret, yearning

ITS PURPOSE IS TO...

Allow us to imagine things or people we'd like to have close to us

THE TIME ORIENTATION OF THIS EMOTION IS...

Past

HOW THIS EMOTION CAN GET IN THE WAY

Wistfulness informs us of things we loved and appreciated in our past. We can use this to create our present and future, but living in the mood of wistfulness keeps us stuck in a past that no longer exists.

EMOTIONS WE CONFUSE IT WITH

Yearning. Yearning is wanting something so badly it hurts that we cannot have it. Wistfulness is recalling something from the past that was deeply meaningful to us.

HOW IT FEELS OR MOVES US

To dream about a different life

HOW OUR BODY MIGHT FEEL

Slow and lethargic

HOW OUR BREATH MIGHT BE

Exhales longer than inhales, often with a sigh

HOW OUR BODY MIGHT SHAPE ITSELF

Perhaps the shoulders are a bit stooped

QUOTE

"We all feel wistfulness or regret about roads not taken."
—Deborah Tannen

WONDER

ETYMOLOGICAL ROOT

Old English *wundor*, "marvelous thing, miracle, object of astonishment"

WHAT WE THINK OR SAY

"Amazing!" "This is beyond any experience I've ever had (in a good way)."

ITS IMPACT ON OUR OPENNESS TO OTHERS

Opens us

OUR REACTION OR IMPULSE FOR ACTION IS...

To continue in the experience

RELATED EMOTIONS

Awe, amazement, incredulity

ITS PURPOSE IS TO...

Connect us with things in the world bigger and more powerful than we are

THE TIME ORIENTATION OF THIS EMOTION IS...

Present

HOW THIS EMOTION CAN GET IN THE WAY

Wonder takes us away from everyday concerns but can also disconnect or unground us from the day-to-day actions of life.

EMOTIONS WE CONFUSE IT WITH

Awe is similar to wonder but includes an element of fear or intimidation that wonder does not.

HOW IT FEELS OR MOVES US

Slack-jawed, open-mouthed, wide-eyed, looking up, body forward

HOW OUR BODY MIGHT FEEL

Tingling, goose bumps

HOW OUR BREATH MIGHT BE

Stopped

HOW OUR BODY MIGHT SHAPE ITSELF

Fully open, eyes wide, head up, chest full front and back, a sense of moving up in space

QUOTE

"The sea, once it casts its spell, holds one in its net of wonder forever."—Jacques Yves Cousteau

YEARNING

ETYMOLOGICAL ROOT

Old English *giernan*, "to strive, be eager, desire, seek for, beg, demand"

WHAT WE THINK OR SAY

"I have a tremendous desire to fill an emptiness I feel."

ITS IMPACT ON OUR OPENNESS TO OTHERS

Opens us

OUR REACTION OR IMPULSE FOR ACTION IS…

To profoundly desire

RELATED EMOTIONS

Wistfulness, desire, passion

ITS PURPOSE IS TO…

Know what we want most profoundly

THE TIME ORIENTATION OF THIS EMOTION IS…

Future

HOW THIS EMOTION CAN GET IN THE WAY

If we live in yearning, we may never take action on the opportunities right in front of us because we are dreaming of something that is not available.

EMOTIONS WE CONFUSE IT WITH

Desire. To yearn is to want something so badly that we feel pain if we can't have it. Desire is the wish for something to become available to us.

HOW IT FEELS OR MOVES US

To long for, wish for, desire and search for

HOW OUR BODY MIGHT FEEL

Being pulled towards the desired state or thing; maybe some tension in the belly and chest

HOW OUR BREATH MIGHT BE

Long, slow, deep breaths

HOW OUR BODY MIGHT SHAPE ITSELF

Depth and width diminish somewhat and allow for greater length

QUOTE

"Give me your tired, your poor, your huddled masses yearning to breathe free."—Emma Lazarus

ZEAL

The emotion is............................

ETYMOLOGICAL ROOT

From Greek *zelos*, "ardor, eager rivalry, emulation; a noble passion"

WHAT WE THINK OR SAY

"I can't wait!"

ITS IMPACT ON OUR OPENNESS TO OTHERS

Opens us

OUR REACTION OR IMPULSE FOR ACTION IS...

To engage with tremendous energy

RELATED EMOTIONS

Excitement, enthusiasm, passion

ITS PURPOSE IS TO...

Put us into energetic action

THE TIME ORIENTATION OF THIS EMOTION IS...

Present

HOW THIS EMOTION CAN GET IN THE WAY

To be overzealous means we are so focused on what we want to achieve that we miss what is happening around us or alienate those we want to include.

EMOTIONS WE CONFUSE IT WITH

Ambition. Ambition means we see possibilities and want to go get them. Zeal means to act out of passion and with great energy, but is not necessarily concerned with capturing opportunities.

HOW IT FEELS OR MOVES US

We jump into action with delight.

HOW OUR BODY MIGHT FEEL

Energized, strong

HOW OUR BREATH MIGHT BE

High in the chest, rapid pace

HOW OUR BODY MIGHT SHAPE ITSELF

Moving forward, length, width, and depth all balanced

QUOTE

"My candle burns at both ends; It will not last the night; But ah, my foes, and oh, my friends—It gives a lovely light!"—Edna St. Vincent Millay

327

CONCLUSION

We hope that this volume has been and will continue to be useful in your exploration of emotions and that you are able to become more effective as a result of reading and applying it.

As we stated at the beginning of this book, this is our interpretation of how one might begin to look at and participate in one's emotional life. We mean it truly to be a starting place of exploration for the reader, not a destination or definitive truth.

The very nature of emotions only allows us to witness and practice in the territory of emotional intelligence, never to reach a place of "this is what it is"; and for us, this is both the challenge and the fun of it. We hope you are challenged and have fun as well.

In gratitude,
Dan and Curtis

ABOUT THE AUTHORS

Curtis Watkins has spent his life being curious about why things are the way they are, and so he became a chronic learner, following his heart's desire: acting in NYC, driving a cab, waiting on tables, bartending, hitch-hiking a bunch, working construction, being one of the first male flight attendants for TWA, world traveler, hiker, husband, father, business failure, divorcee, EST and Lifespring graduate, Somatic and Ontological Coach, and lots more. The thread throughout all these experiences has been a mood of curiosity which led to much exploration and adventure. This book is in that line—an exploration of emotions and the body. He hopes you enjoy the journey.

Dan Newby learned early in life that learning was a privilege and never a waste of time or effort. This belief led him to train as a teacher, travel widely, live in many different parts of the U.S. and other countries, work at many levels within organizations, start businesses, become a coach, and finally land in Spain, which he considers home. Along with his wife he wrote *The Unopened Gift*, which is a reframing of emotions using a practical and logical interpretation. He is a cook, gardener, and he loves wandering in new places. He hopes this exploration of emotions is enlightening, enjoyable, and promotes your learning in a new domain.

RESOURCES/MORE INFORMATION

Please feel free to contact Curtis or Dan through LinkedIn or at these email addresses:

Curtis Watkins: cwatkosmic@aol.com

Dan Newby: dan@dannewby.me

OUR WORK

Books: Dan is co-author of the book *"The Unopened Gift: A Primer in Emotional Literacy."* It is available in Spanish as *"Emociones: Un Regalo por Abrir: Introducción a la Alfabetización Emocional."* There is an accompanying workbook titled "21 Days to Emotional Literacy" available in English and Spanish. All are available worldwide on Amazon and Kindle.

Workshops: We offer workshops several times a year for coaches who would like to deepen their understanding of emotions and learn ways to use emotions as a tool to increase the effectiveness of their coaching. If this idea is of interest to you, please write us.

Coaching: Both authors offer individual coaching. We have experience working with executives and managers at all levels and from many cultural backgrounds. Coaching can take place in person or through video conferencing.

Coach Mentoring: We offer mentoring for coaches, whether for certification renewal or to enhance skills. These sessions can be individual or group. They are generally done by video conference but can be arranged in person.

Facilitation: Both authors have a long history of facilitation for groups, particularly in leadership development and emotions. We offer programs customized to the needs of your team or organization.

Online Training: Dan offers online training in Emotional Literacy for coaches, leaders, parents, and teachers. These programs are asynchronous and can be accessed through any Internet connection. Additional information and a list of courses is available at www.studyemotions.com. For online programs focused on the aviation sector, please visit www.safetyrelations.com.

ACKNOWLEDGMENTS

We would like to acknowledge the work of Richard Strozzi-Heckler and the Strozzi Institute in the field of somatics, from which we have drawn the distinctions of Length, Width, and Depth that are used in this book. Length is the vertical axis from head to toe and can be associated with the domain of accomplishment: having a vision and the ability to carry out a vision. Width is the horizontal axis stretching from fingertip to fingertip across the chest at the heart level and can be associated with the social domain: the ability to engage with the world without being overwhelmed by it and without trying to dominate it. Depth is the dimension of front body to back body and can be related to one's connection to the past, tradition, family, and ancestors. For further information on these distinctions, we recommend you read Dr. Heckler's book *"Holding the Center."*

Printed in Great Britain
by Amazon

48307661R00200